THE OCCULT OF UNIVERSE

LAW OF UNIVERSE

SIMRAN ASHISH SINGH

This is my second book and this book is dedicated to my husband because people say that the life of girls changes completely after marriage, but it did not happen to me, in fact, he always told me to go ahead regardless of anything, I always stand by you.

And

Specially thanks to my loving didi and Maa Papa. without you, this journey was not possible for me.

Contents

Preface

First of all I would like to write that why I am writing this book. I was fighting my self for last two years in all the fields even if it family, job, study, love, I was feel like everything loosing in my hand nothing is in my control. I was totally gone on depression.

But it is said that when all the roads are closed, then God definitely opens a way. One day I was scrolling my phone and I got the pdf of the Gita book, I started reading, when I kept reading, I understood that nothing is away from us, we make such a mind that Everything is over, I have learned that no one can defeat us until we lose ourselves. And if we are determined to do something, then the universe will also It may take us long to introduce him, just to trust us. And then what was it, I too will lose my promise to myself, daily start doing a little work for myself, Ignore everyone's talk, just do what my own heart said And today everything is my family job love everything. thanks to god and law of universe.

Acknowledgements

To God for your loving guidance and for the many blessings you have bestwishes upon me to my family maa. papa, didi, jiju, chotu thanks for your love and support and for the code of ethics you thought me which has served me so well in my life.

To my special thanks to my husband, for your enthusiastic support of my work and encouragement and guidance without you this is not possible to me.

Prologue

Because, for starters, these laws are what have been the basis of everything—from the tiniest atom to the largest sun—everything has stemmed from these laws. And these laws only give way to what is already in our minds. It is believed that the one who understands each of these laws to their fullest is the one to hold the key to the mystery of life; to being the Master of this Universe. And truth is, some of our ancient philosophers and thinkers believed and implemented these laws in their lives; which is why they were perpetually content and grateful for everything they ever received; because they were manifesting everything into their lives with their mere thoughts. Your thoughts are not just powerful; they're the key to your life. And it is only proven true by these laws.

CHAPTER ONE

THE LAW OF DIVINE ONENESS

> *"Oneness is inner silence, which remains undisturbed by external factors. This silence is not the opposite of noise. That is inner oneness. – Kalki Bhagavan"*

The law states that everything is connected to everything else. What we think, say, do, or believe will have a corresponding effect on others, as well as the Universe around us. According to the law, all of humanity and God are one. The energy of God is everywhere all at once and it flows through everything—living, or inanimate. Each soul is said to be part of God's energy.

Ever heard the saying that there is a little bit of God in all of us? That God made us be images of his own self? It's because of this law. Everything that exists—both, seen or unseen—is connected to everything. When we become aware of this law and believe that everything is one, the way we think and act with respect to everyone and everything around us will change. We will see our own reflection in the people and things around us. It means that the more good we think about others, the better it comes back to us and becomes us. Everything in this Universe is made up of energy—you, your friend, your enemy, the chair you sit on, the laptop you work on and the phone you make calls on. And this energy is what governs the movement of everything in this Universe.

Law of Divine Oneness is the reason why spiritual growth is so important. As we learn and grow, we learn how if we're all connected, setting our vibrational frequency higher and higher can have an extremely positive influence on our hive mind. If inside of you there is pain, sadness, anger and turmoil, fear of rejection, hatred, and so on that is what you are feeding to the collective, which in turn brings down others and as a whole affects the hive mind negatively. When you operate at a higher frequency, such as peace, joy, and love you are feeding that vibrational frequency to the collective consciousness. You are bringing a positive vibration to the collective consciousness.

This is why group mediations are so beneficial to the collective. Meditating in general helps you to center yourself and align with source energy, finding the creative and free source you have allowed society to bury and suffocate within you.

It's the root, or the anchor, that is at the end of our collective tether within you.

We are all affected by each other's vibrational frequency, however, there is an element of projection involved as well. I'm sure many of you have noticed this phenomenon, where your attitude directly lines up with how and what situations unfold before your eyes. Your energetic vibration in a situation typically correlates with the outcome. If you go out into society with a bad mood and a lower vibration, you not only will continue to create more of that energy, see more of that energy (this also involves our reticular activating system), and affect others negatively.

To sum it all up, you will typically get what you are expecting. If you are expecting fear, that's what you will get. Our emotions help create our perspective of our living experience. If you expect love, you will get more love. Even if someone is trying to give you love, but you expect rejection, you aren't allowing yourself to be open to receiving that love. You subconsciously have that setting turned off, you are projecting rejection and that's what you will receive back in return.

If you can control your thoughts, you can ultimately create your destiny and optimally change your reality.

One really cool thing about your brain is that the subconscious mind does not know the difference between reality and dreams. If you believe that something is, you can begin to rewire your brain and your subconscious mind to what you desire and who you want to become.

If you are a victim of a traumatic incident, our brains typically tend to replay that horrific event in our minds. From my understanding, it acts as a part of our fight or flight response to help us not let that happen again.

If you only allow negative thoughts, feelings, and emotions to play out in your mind your subconscious believes those negative things are really happening on a molecular level.

Dr. Joe Dispenza wrote a book called "Becoming Supernatural" which talks about how we can actually heal ourselves with our minds. If we can heal ourselves, and I am you, I can help to heal you as well. Much like a prayer, sending a message to God, when meditating you can send someone else in the collective healing energy and divine light. When thinking of anyone throughout the day, be sure to send them love and light, (i.e positive vibes). On some level, you are literally sending them energy that (if they are open to it) they are receiving! Women typically tend to be more intuitive. This is why they tend to be more inclined to be an empath and why they seem to be more receptive to everyone's emotions.

The Law of Divine Oneness is foundational in understanding the other 11 Universal Laws. They are all intertwined. Like one perfect formula we have deduced as humans to be the key to understanding the universe. Everything is energy. Everything is a vibration. Everything is operating at a certain frequency. And if we can learn how to control our particular frequency and manipulate it for the better, we can begin to ascend to the next level of consciousness.

Understanding the Law of Divine Oneness

The feeling you get when you understand the Law of Divine Oneness is unlike anything else. When you know how this Law affects the way we live, you'll change the way you approach life.

You'll live in a feel-good mood most of the time because you understand why certain things happen. You stop blaming yourself and others. You'll increase your life success and be more conscious of your contribution to the world.

The Law of Divine Oneness teaches that you are a part of the whole made up of everything else around you.

Fun fact: The human cellular makeup has elements that resemble some aspects of the solar system.

The solar system might not be living per se, but sharing an element with it is proof that it is part of us. Think of the cycle of life. You are born, you grow old to the end of your time on earth. And as the saying goes, dust becomes dust. In other words, you return to the earth from which you came.

It is that same ground that we grow our food on and from which our plants get their nutrients. Essentially, the connection we have on earth finds its way back to us in one form or the other. But it goes beyond the physical.

Law of Oneness Meaning

The Law of Oneness brings harmony to all Life Laws. The Law of Oneness teaches that we are all linked. A concept that the Law of Cause and Effect also supports. We all share the same energy.

According to the two Laws, it is because of the connection between our energies that we 'feel' each other. We might not recognize these occurrences as instances of the Universal Laws. Yet once you know these laws, those occurrences are proof that these laws work.

Take, for instance, how a parent gets a feeling that their child is in trouble, and it turns out to be true. Or how you might avoid a particular favorite route, then receive news later that something terrible happened along that route. Or when you call a friend or loved one, and immediately they pick up, they tell you that they were just about to contact you!

It might all look like luck or a coincidence, but once you take a closer look, you realize that nothing is random. Multiple universal energies influence and are influenced by our actions, thoughts, and feelings. Unfortunately, when we don't realize that we exist as a whole and not as individuals, we tilt the universal balance.

Where there should be order, chaos thrives.

Places where there should be love, hatred flourishes.

Where there should be community, individualism blooms.

Breaking the Laws of the Universe forms the foundation for unexplained and unwanted manifestations. Yet, our misunderstanding of these Laws makes us believe that whatever happens around us is normal. Listen to people's explanations of events, and you'll hear a synonymous belief that "that's life."Actually, that's life without knowing the Universal Life Laws. When you know these Laws, you control and improve your life.

Atonement vs.Oneness vs. At-one-ment (At one ment)

Call it atonement, Oneness, or at-one-ment. The bottom line is that it all circles back to one thing – our ability to return to a harmonious existence where we work for the whole. In other words, Oneness is about contributing to the universe in ways that are beneficial not only to us but to all that's around us.

Think about it. Today, there are only a few hundred companies that are responsible for the most pollution across the world. As those behind these companies line their pockets, the world continues to suffer. Destruction of animal habitats, plastic pollution, oil spills, and the release of toxic gases into the environment are only examples of the effects of the lack of Oneness with the world.

Logging has also had adverse effects on the ecology and environment. This points to a lack of Oneness, love, and harmony in the world. So, what is happening now? Many of these companies are seeking atonement, meaning they are paying to correct the effects of pollution.

So, what is happening now? Many of these companies are seeking atonement, meaning they are paying to correct the effects of pollution. The only thing left to do to regain Oneness with the universe is practice atonement. But what is the definition of atonement, at-one-ment (at one ment), Oneness, and are they different?

Oneness

The state or fact of being unified or whole, though comprised of two or more parts.

Atonement

Living in a state of feeling one with everything and everyone, knowing not to judge someone because you have the same thing in you. It may appear different, but it's the same. For example, someone may judge an alcoholic. A close look in the mirror of at one ment would show them that they have trouble handling money, or overeating, or working too much, or have some other challenge with self-control.

We might see someone do something foolish and judge them. Yet, we make mistakes; every one of us does. So should we be judging others when we are all the same? Or should we understand? Because we are what they are. That would be living in a state of at-one-ment. How peaceful would that be? Those who know the Law of Oneness live in that calm state, and it's easy to do.

Atonement

Reparation for a wrong or injury.

Going by the atonement definition above and that of Oneness, atonement is what we do when we want to reconcile our wrongdoings. Essentially, atonement is the action taken to get back in sync and correct a fall out with the whole.

The Law of One is the only way to find your place.

Understanding the Law of One is the only way to find your place in the whole. It will also help you align your life and actions to be in sync with the universe. The Law of One helps us realize that we are all part of one energy force. Which means you are more significant than you think.

Every creation has a connection to this universal energy, although we often feel disconnected. To connect and realize a state of Oneness, it is helpful to tune into our higher self.

How do we tune into our higher self?

One of the most potent ways of tuning into our spirituality is through meditation. By meditating, we allow universal energy to communicate with us. The communication can be through a voice in the mind, thoughts, feelings, and even a physical voice. Still, many of us struggle with being at one with the world even though we all have in us that same energy. Connecting with this energy and realizing Oneness raises our energy and vibrations. In turn, our health, happiness, and satisfaction improve tremendously. So do our joy and contentedness in ourselves.

At One Ment Brings a Reformed World-View

What happens when we are in at one ment, is that we start working together and helping each other. We begin taking responsibility for what we project and physically do to the world and each other. We automatically and effortlessly start becoming the best version of ourselves. But as you work towards understanding the Law of Oneness, it's crucial that you also seek to understand the other Universal Laws. You can then start connecting the dots and discovering how they intersect.

As mentioned before, you'll realize that when one Law is neglected, the effectiveness of the other Laws suffers. Ultimately, it goes to show that these Laws might be separate, but they are part of a whole and in at-one-ment with each other. If only the world's population would be aware of the principals of these Laws. Then, we would be content with our lives, have an abundance mindset, love each other, and be consciously united.

Eventually, being aware of the power of the Universal Laws chips away at our disconnect. As our disconnection disappears, the reconnection in its place fosters Oneness. The fact is that energy for good, love, and light exists in each one of us. But the war, illnesses, poverty, hatred, and racism that is rife across the world suppress our ability to believe that we can make an impact.

However, we have the free will to decide how we allow circumstances to affect us. It is through free will that we can also choose what to believe. After creation, we had choices. Choices to preserve the world and maintain its original balance, or to let our individuality lead us. The state of the world today shows that we chose the latter, causing imbalance and separating ourselves from the universe and each other.

What We Should Learn from The Law of Divine Oneness

The most important takeaways from understanding the Law of Divine Oneness are:

1. We Are Not Separate Entities

All things in the universe have a link to each other. Our existence is like a circle, and it is impossible to live a solitary life. Our Collective Consciousness and shared universal energy bind us to everyone and everything.

2. Everything We Do Has an Effect on The World

Thoughts. Actions. Words. Beliefs. All of these have an impact on us as individuals and on our Collective Conscience and existence. The significance of this is that you influence the type of life you lead and your circumstances.

You have the control of whether you live a miserable judgmental, or understanding joyous life. Whatever you dedicate your mind and thoughts to is what you manifest. If you entertain thoughts of scarcity and poverty, you create these situations. If you harbor thoughts of abundance, wealth, and good health, you attract them into your life.

Suppose you said hurtful words to someone. Does it stop there? No. That person becomes sad or angry or anxious. Most likely, they won't be their bubbly self around co-workers or their family. Now the energy around the work office and home are more suppressed. And that is if they aren't crying or lashing out because then it's worse than only suppressed! That energy affects others at work and home. Then how do your co-workers feel, and how will they interact with others? And how about those others? And the next ones? Probably not in a positive, happy way. The energy gets lower in the office. And this continues with a ripple effect, on and on. What appears to affect one affects everything.

By shifting our thoughts, beliefs, words, and actions, we can influence our reality. You can start this by focusing on what you want rather than dwelling on what you don't want.

3. Our Collective Consciousness is a Powerhouse

Collective Consciousness means this universal energy that connects us. We are all conscious, so together, we make up the Collective Consciousness. The inventions the world has seen have become a reality because of one thing – they are a manifestation of people's desires. The more people with similar thoughts, the easier and faster these thoughts become a reality.

And these are usually based on something that someone else created. The car – came after someone invented the wheel, engines, gears, and more. And all those things came after someone came up with something else such as mining metals to make some of these parts, creating rubber, cloth, refining fuels, etc. And we can go back and back.

What goes into a chair? The nails someone invented using the metal someone else mined. The wood that someone cut from the forest and another cut into lumber and another shaped for the chair. The glue that someone processed and the container it was in that someone created and processed. Varnish, sandpaper, saws, hammers, transporting the items, the list goes on. And what was one of the first parts of the Collective Conscience that created the chair, the car, and everything to make them – an idea.

Hopefully, you don't ever look at things the same again. Everything is a masterpiece from the concept – through to the creation. One person couldn't do this alone, so it took the Collective Consciousness. Things are created because of the Law of Oneness. Next to nothing could exist without Oneness.

These are two examples of billions of things and ideas coming from the Collective Consciousness – from all of us. We all have a duty as part of this Collective Conscience. Think of any successful invention. You'll realize that it has one driving factor– people's interest in finding a better way to accomplish something. This Collective Conscience triggers a light bulb moment in an individuals' brain. That energy leads several connected people to a path of inventing to satisfy a common need/desire.

Final Thoughts

We benefit from becoming aware of our thoughts and being strategic with our speech/utterings and actions. They all have an impact on the entire world.

Awareness of our impact on our environment will keep us from amplifying the suffering in the world. In its place, it will intensify healing and our contribution towards improving universal Oneness. Today, since many are unaware of the Universal Laws, the depletion of the earth's resources and wars prevail.

At some point, the earth may be in grave danger. Without a choice, nature and the earth itself will force us to go back to our roots and go through a period of atonement. Then will we reconnect to our Oneness and facilitate the healing and regeneration of earth's resources and peace among men. Let's hope this doesn't have to happen.

CHAPTER TWO

LAW OF VIBRATON

"*Nothing rests;*
everything moves;
everything vibrates.
-The Kybalion"

Everything in the universe is in motion, whether solid, liquid, or gas. All things move, vibrate, and travel in circular patterns. Each thing that exists is identical by its own unique vibrational frequency. Frequency is defined as the number of periodic oscillations, vibrations, or waves per unit of time.

No two things in the universe are truly identical, because each has its unique vibrational pattern. The differences between matter and energy are explained primarily by the differences in these vibratory motions. Phenomena such as light, heat, magnetism, electricity, and sound are forms of vibratory motion, just as trees, desks, flowers, and animals are.

When things vibrate very slowly, we hear no noise. Physical objects vibrate slowest, which is why we cannot hear any sounds emanating from them. As vibration is increased, we begin to hear lower-pitched sounds. Further increases in vibration allow us to hear higher-pitched notes, as when we strike the ascending keys of the piano. If vibrations increase further, to a higher frequency, we may not be able to hear the sound because it may have moved out of our ability to register the frequency.

So it is with our ability to see color. We are limited in seeing only the colors that are contained within the spectrum of Light – the rainbow. Our first perception of color is dark red. As vibrations increase, the red becomes brighter, then turns to orange, and then to yellow, green blue, indigo, and violet. Violet vibrates higher into ultraviolet where we no longer have the ability to see the color, just as we cannot see infrared with the naked eye.

The same principles of vibration that apply to the physical world also apply to us and to our thoughts, feelings, desires, and will. We each have our own unique sound say the Ascended Masters, and that perfect sound is who we really are. If we would become still long enough to connect with this sound, we would discover our true, perfect selves.

Disruptions in our lives, our lifestyles, television, radio, people, and noises, in general, all serve to keep us from hearing that perfect sound within and from becoming it. Many of the vibrational frequencies in the world work to compete with and disrupt our mental and emotional states, keeping us from connecting with the perfection lying dormant inside.

Our thoughts, emotions, and will send out vibrations into the universe. Every thought or mental state has a corresponding rate and mode of vibration. The higher the vibration, the longer-lasting the effects are. The lower the vibration, the more potent the effects are in the short term.

The Law of Vibration is considered to be "what is." In these dimensions, nothing is assigned meaning, only a frequency. Thoughts, emotions, behaviors, and actions are understood for the level at which they reside. An angry person is analyzed objectively as being angry, with no value assigned to the behavior. An effort is made to try and understand the behavior, and perhaps a plan is prepared to try and raise the vibrational frequency to a higher level, thus transmuting the anger into something less painful.

We live in the Third Dimension, the plane of dichotomies, which reflects most things as good/bad, black/white, or yes/no. Because our identity is associated with this mode of operation, most of us have a characteristic style of optimism or pessimism. Optimism resides on a higher frequency and pessimism resides on a lower frequency. Optimists tend to expect more of the world. This is communicated to others and is likely to be realized. Pessimists expect the negative. They anticipate gloom and doom and actually help to create it. Our basic style is important because whatever we choose creates a vibration that goes out into the collective consciousness and helps whether to raise Earth's vibrations or to lower them. When we express negativity, we take on an amount of negativity equal to what we have expressed. Similarly, when we express ourselves in positive ways, we take on an equal amount of positive vibrations.

Vibrations not only affect us but also impact the people around us. Positive or negative vibrations may resonate in others and create similar vibrations. If we send out thoughts of envy, criticism, hatred, or jealousy, then the same thought forms are aroused and sent back by others.

Each of us has the power to choose. We can align our bodies and our behaviors to create harmony and consistency with the God within us. Just as we care for our bodies by choosing options and behaviors – food, exercise, freedom from addictions – to maintain our balance and remain in a state of health, we also must take care of our minds by choosing good thoughts. Positive thoughts help us move on our journey to spiritual development. Other thoughts inhibit our progress or cause us to regress. When we learn to choose the good, we move toward spiritual goals with measured progress.

Often, the full impact of our behavior on others is not well understood. We can be a positive force working for the betterment of our organization or community, or we can be a negative force and tear down what is being built. Perhaps the most difficult form of negativity to overcome is personal or group cynicism. Many individuals who have experienced multiple disappointments or failures begin to believe that nothing will work. The group mind then creates a vibrational frequency that draws to these individuals everything else that resides on that frequency. In order to solve their problems, the individuals must learn to open their minds and hearts and think from a place connected to higher consciousness, for the solutions will be found only on the higher planes of existence. Through the Law of Vibration, this most of behavior always brings the answer we are seeking, for the higher frequencies contain greater knowledge and wisdom.

A few try to rationalize their negativity by saying that they need to be honest. When people are motivated to behave in a negative way, however, the vibrational frequency emitted speaks for itself. We need to strive to be honest and helpful and still be positive.

Our goal is to keep our vibrations as positive and as high as possible. This means that we must not let another's negative attitudes penetrate our feelings or mental state. One of the ways to accomplish this is to learn to keep from becoming overly involved in the problems of others. We need to listen carefully, help establish goals for solving problems, and assist in planning positive outcomes, but we must keep ourselves from taking on the lower vibrations emitted by others.

Understanding the Law of Vibration assists us to get in touch with our feelings every moment of the day. Since each thought, feeling, word, and behavior resides on its own frequency, we need to learn to assess how we feel and to choose behaviors and attitudes that only help us evolve. Evolution is why we are here. The Law of Vibration gives us the basis of knowledge to transcend all that is not in the Divine plan and provides us the way to move to higher planes of existence.

The Law of Vibration states that nothing is ever static. Everything in this Universe whether visible or unseen broken down and analyzed under a powered microscope will show to consist of finer particles that pulsate in a particular pattern. Furthermore, our thoughts and feelings are also energy. Therefore, when you think good thoughts you are vibrating in a "positive" vibration.

On the other hand, when you are feeling low, you are vibrating in "negative" emotions. Synchronized vibrations will connect together and will result in wonderful manifestations. Most importantly, the brain acts as a vibratory switching station. We use our brain to interpret our life situations and then allow it to switch our entire being to a particular vibration.

THE SCIENCE BEHIND THE LAW OF VIBRATION

There is a scientific explanation behind this law. Quantum science gives us the explanation that nothing is static in this world.

Quantum Physics postulates that each and every particle that exists in our universe is made of energy. Microscopic studies have proved that matter is composed of finer molecules and atoms.

Also, these finer particles are vibrating at a certain rate of vibration. This has been established through scientific studies. Samples of bacteria or the human skin, for instance, have been seen to be composed of finer particles rotating at high speed.

Considering the Law of Vibration from a Spiritual Perspective

From a spiritual perspective, everything is a part of a Higher Power or Source energy or Universe Consciousness. The source of energy connects us through our Subconscious mind. Our energy vibrations help us to remain deeply connected to this Universal Consciousness or get disconnected to it.

This is why vibes are so important. Therefore, when in a high vibe you will maintain this connection, again a prolonged low vibe can disconnect it.

Vibrational manifestation

"If you want to find the secrets of the universe, think in terms of energy, frequency and vibration."

— Nikola Tesla

Everything is energy. We are all energy beings vibrating at individual frequencies. This is a concept beyond human consciousness. Even our thoughts, feelings, words, and actions all constitute energy. To think of, we are entities consisting of energy packets vibrating at all times. Now, the thoughts we think and the emotions we feel enable us to vibrate at a certain frequency level.

When we are vibrating at a certain level we would attract situations, people, resources, and stuff that are vibrating at this frequency level. According to the Law of Attraction, like attracts like.

According to the Law of Vibration, you will bring into your life circumstances, people, etc. that resonates with your frequency. So, if you are feeling miserable you will attract more miserable people and situations in life.

If you are always fearful, you will be a strong magnet that draws fearful incidents towards them. Similarly, if you are always happy you will bring more reasons in your life to be happy about.

This is how synchronized vibrations happen. Simply put, positive vibration attracts positive vibration and negative vibration attracts negative vibration. If you keep your vibration at a higher frequency you will always attract great things in your life.

This is how energy flows and manifestations happen. The concept of vibrational manifestation is that when you intentionally vibrate at a higher frequency you would be able to manifest or create the life you want!

Everything is Vibration

All particles in this Universe are resonating at a certain frequency. Nothing is ever resting. Even if you see an object lying still in front of you, know that all its particles are vibrating at high speed.

If you observe it through a high-resolution microscope you would be able to see that all of its constituent particles are rotating in different vibrations. So, you can simply say that everything is constantly in motion or everything is vibration.

Benefits of the Law of Vibration

Your vibration sets your reality. If you are not satisfied with the results you are getting in life, you must consciously choose to change your vibrational frequency! You can do it simply by focusing on a positive idea.

As you start to raise your vibration you will start to attract similar vibrations in your conscious awareness. Therefore, you will become a magnet to the success, prosperity, and experiences that you desire. Simply put, you will become the designer of your life.

How to use the Law of Vibration in your favor?

The Personal Development Gurus are making millions of dollars teaching on this subject. But we are giving you certain easy and effective ways to use the law of vibration, absolutely free!

The 10 easiest ways to use the Law of Vibration are –

1. Gratitude

The simplest way to raise your vibe is by expressing gratitude. You can do it mentally, out loud or jot down in a journal. Whenever you shower your gratitude towards things you have in your life, your vibrational energy goes higher up.

As a result, your thoughts, feelings, and actions start to become better and you start manifesting wonderful things in your life.

2. Speak Positively

Whenever you have disempowering thoughts and emotions, do this. For each negative thought say 5 positive statements in your mind. This cancels the negative idea and reprograms the subconscious mind. Most importantly, make positive self-talk a habit.

You can use your conscious mind to impress positive ideas to the Subconscious. As you consciously choose positivity in your life, you become a high vibrational being.

Change your vibration by speaking out strong, happy, and empowering words.

Negative words (Eliminate such words from your dictionary)

Positive words (Start using such statements from now on)

1. **I am not well. I am awesome!**
2. **I can't do it. Yes, I can do it!**
3. **I have such bad luck. I am an extremely lucky person!**
4. **I don't think you can do that. Try again, I am sure you can do that!**

5. **I don't trust people anymore. I believe there are many good people out there.**

Did she get a promotion? No way! She doesn't deserve it. Wow, she got a promotion! So happy for her. She deserves it!

3. Eat High-Vibe Food

The food you eat nourishes both your body and mind. Green vegetables, fruits, fresh foods, clean water has high vibes in them. On the other hand, stale foods, meat, foods with preservatives and artificial colors are low-vibe foods, therefore, try to avoid those.

Therefore, make a habit of eating fresh and healthy foods because it will increase your vibration. You can easily find out how food creates a specific vibration in your body. The food that makes you feel good from within is a high vibe food.

4. Stop Gossiping

Whenever you utter something nasty about someone even secretly, you immediately start emitting negative energy. We are energy beings and all of us are connected to the Source of energy. Therefore, even if you remark something negative at someone's back the energy flows to the person and is felt. They too unconsciously give you back the negative vibe and you remain in this circle forever. Most importantly, if you always want to stay in a high vibe stop saying bad things about others. Be careful about your words because they have an effect on your energy frequency. Gossiping and backbiting never help anyone, only it brings negativity in your mind and your environment.

5. Smile Often

Laughter has several benefits. It can heal you and it can raise your energy in an instant. You really don't need a reason to smile!

6. Match your vibration with your desires

If you want something, match your vibration to that level. Bring similar energies in your life or put yourself to that kind of energy. So, if you want to become healthy, start storing fresh fruits and veggies in your refrigerator. If you want to become a musician buy a guitar or even better join a class.

7. Surround yourself with higher vibrations

> "*"You are the average of the five people you spend the most time with."*
> *--Jim Rohn*"

You will always be the average of your closest pals. Whether you like this piece of information or not, you can never excel if you stay in an environment of mediocrity. If you want to use the Law of Vibration and become a successful person, start networking with high-vibration people.

Interact with people who are doing much more than what you are doing in your present life. When you raise your vibration it is the quickest way to shift your vibration and change your life.

8. Use a vision board

Google pictures that reflect your ideal life. What kind of house do you want to live in, what car do you want to drive, what is your ideal lifestyle, what kind of friends do you see yourself hanging around with? Be very specific and download all such pictures that reflect your ideal life.

Now here's the thing! This has nothing to do with the current life you are living or your situation at the present moment. No. Download all pictures that represent your dream life.

Now take a printout of these pictures, cut and arrange them and paste all those pictures on a poster board. This is called a vision board. You have to place this vision board somewhere you would be able to see frequently all day long. This is one of the effective ways to get into a higher frequency.

The more you see your dream life you start vibrating at a higher level. As a result, you start drawing into your life unexpected opportunities that take you towards the life of your desire.

9. Spend time in nature

One of the easiest ways to raise your vibe and use the Law of Vibration in your favor is by spending time alone in nature. The more you put yourself in natural environments the more you raise your vibrational frequency.

Walk on the beach or go mountain trekking. Or you can sit beneath a tree every day to absorb the natural high vibrations.

10. Practice mindfulness

Our mind wanders like a vagabond all the time! Practice mindfulness to focus on your present moment. Meditation is said to improve concentration level. Or you can just keep observing your thoughts. As soon as you find your mind diverting from your current moment, bring it back to focus.

HOW TO APPLY THE LAW OF DIVINE ONENESS

We are extensions of source energy also called God or the Universe. The Law of Divine Oneness, says we are all one with the Universe. You may have heard the statement. We are spiritual beings having a human experience. We are made up of a body, soul, and spirit.

We came into this physical body with a purpose, and that is to grow and evolve. So we embarked on this game. We can call it the game of life, or we can call it the matrix! We are living in a matrix! And just like the matrix, there are rules in how you play the game.

The Rules of the Law of Divine Oneness

The rules are the laws of the Universe. The first Law we will discuss is The Law of Divine Oneness.
If you are a bible scholar you will recognize lots of parallels between the laws of the Universe, and the teachings of, Jesus.
Jesus, came into his physical body with the awareness that he was a subset of God or God incarnate in the flesh. He understood The Law of Divine Oneness.

We are also a subset of God, that is why man can command diseases to leave the body and perform the same miracles, Jesus did on the earth. Jesus, the most profound scripture tells us.

"“If we have the faith as small as a mustard seed, we can command the mountain to move into the sea.”

I bet you have never seen anyone do that in the natural, but in the, matrix, you can! In Higher consciousness you can. I have heard of monks elevating their bodies and travelling from one place to another."

Blanco

Universal Law, The Law of Divine Oneness

The Law of Divine Oneness means that we are all connected to one source. Everything we do effects the collective consciousness of the entire, universe.
That is why when we contribute to others and in some way make their lives better, it gives us the highest joy. The bible teaches that it is better to give than to receive and that is because when we give when we share what we have, it makes us feel good.
That is also why the word, Namaste, is so powerful. It means I see the divine in you. Put another way is, I see God's light in you. We are all God's children.

We all originated from one energy, called the source. The Law of Divine Oneness, Everything in this Universe is made up of energy. The bed you sleep in, the TV you watch, the rocks in your garden, the car you drive and most importantly your thoughts. This energy is vibrating

in circular patterns.
Visualize a Ferris wheel. You start off at the bottom and circle to the top and then you are back to where you started. You can get off or you can continue circling in a continuous loop. This is the same as energy. It is circling and whatever we send out is what we will get back.

Even though every object or thing is made up of energy, this energy is vibrating at different frequencies for each thing or object. Your positive thoughts for instance are vibrating at the highest frequency, while your negative thoughts are vibrating at a lower frequency. Just like light envelops darkness, your positive feelings and emotions can eat up your negativity and bad feelings. So always look for the higher vibrations of positive thoughts and feelings.
Now we can take this further. If you attach the energy of emotion to your thoughts, it multiplies your energy. This leads to a quicker harvest or manifestation. Think of it as a super-charged Ferris wheel spinning faster and faster! Your emotions are a good indicator of the frequency you are vibrating. Learn to pay attention to your feelings, they are indications of what you are manifesting either consciously or unconsciously.
Whenever you feel depression, anxiety, or trepidation, it is telling you that you are going in the opposite direction to your destiny.

Everything that exists seen and unseen is connected to each other, inseparable from each other to a field of, divine oneness. Divine all-knowing, the matrix, pure consciousness, or universal mind energy, sometimes also known as Life Force or God. Everything is one.

Increasing awareness of this law will increase our awareness of God and awareness of being connected to everything. It is important for us as a human race to start realizing and understanding this law. As we do, we will realize that what we think of each other should only be for good. As we think of the good in others, they will in turn think of the good in you. It is essential that the thoughts, feeling,s and actions be for good, for we "reap what we sow".

As you gain a fuller understanding of the laws, you will see how they are all related and overlap each other, and govern the world we live in.

Everything consists of and exists as energy. Your subatomic particles aren't fixed, in fact, particles may be flowing into and out of you now from this page, the sky, the floor, your best friend and your worst enemy. In other words, there is no separation. How would you behave if you really knew that you were not separate from life, your friends, colleagues, and every being that has ever existed? The answer is this – probably differently.

CHAPTER THREE

THE LAW OF ACTION

> "*Your positive action combined with positive thinking results in success.*
> *Shiv Khera*"

The Law of Action must be employed in order for us to manifest things on earth. We must engage in actions that support our thoughts dreams, emotions, and words. The Law of action states that you must do the things and perform the actions necessary to achieve what you are setting out to do. Unless you take actions that are in harmony with your thoughts and dreams and proceed in an orderly fashion towards what you want to accomplish, there will be absolutely no foreseeable results. It is here with the law of action that most people falter when pursuing success. It could be their fears or laziness that get in the way.

You can also relate this law to that of the law of cause and effect. The cause is your action, as you take the action there will be a corresponding effect, that of which you may know or only the Universe will know the effect, but there will be an effect. Only by taking actions that correspond with our free will desires will the universe know what to bring into your life. If you wish to learn, then take the action steps to learn - read books, study, etc.. only then will the universe know what you are striving for.

When you take action, from the smallest thing from writing a To-Do list in the morning, you set into motion corresponding effects that change your immediate future, and if you follow up day after day it can become a habitual way of living and the results will be exponential. But if you fail, to take that first action, then there won't be much in your future for results.

It is the actions we take that move us towards our goals and dreams, not only our thoughts and feelings.

Our emotions and thoughts bring the possibilities into our lives and get us onto the right track and into the right frame of mind. The actions are what propel us forward and get us towards the end goal.

The law of action states that we must take action in our lives to see changes happen. Every action we take creates a result.

The law of action also says that if we do nothing, then nothing will happen. It is a beautiful law of the universe that gives us power over our future, and the joy of being a part of the creation of our future.

The Law Of Action And The Law Of Attraction

How does the law of action and the law of attraction complement each other? There are a couple of ways they are interwoven.

First, the law of action acts as the solidifying message to the universe that you want the goal you're going after.

It is one thing to meditate and visualize your future. But unless you take real-world steps towards your goal, it will only ever remain in your mind.

When you move physically towards your goal with an action step, it signifies to the universe that you are willing to get out there and work towards it.

When you do take action, it is incredible how fast things can happen.

Second, when you visualize and set your goals for the future, your mind will start to notice opportunities that will help you reach your end goal.

When you see these opportunities and prompts to take action, you must listen to them. If you do so, you will be taking inspired action that you must learn to understand and trust with your intuition.

When you listen to the signs that are put in front of you, and you act on them, you will start to put yourself in proper situations where you can meet the people you need to meet and be in the places you need to be.

Third, your taking action is your trust and surrender to the process that if you take the necessary steps, you will see things happen for you.

Think about it. If you doubt yourself and are unsure, then you are less likely to take action. However, if you are determined and sure that you will reach your end goal, you are likely to get off the couch and out into the lane leading to your dreams.

CHAPTER FOUR

LAW OF ATTRACTION

> *"The universe is changing, our life is what our thoughts make it."*
> *-Marcus Aurelius.*

Like attracts like, people attract energy like the energy they project. Positive people attract others like them or those moving in the same direction and vice versa. The fact is that you are a magnet. You attract people, ideas, and resources that are in harmony with your dominant thoughts. Thoughts and feelings are energy. Whenever you are sensitive to someone else's feelings, when you are aware of your own feelings, this is a conscious perception of vibration.

Vibration is energy that is either positive or negative. You have the power to choose your thoughts or change them by what you choose to think about, by how you speak to yourself and others. Listen to your thoughts and ask yourself if they are congruent with the person you are or want to be. The energy you project is what you will receive.

You are what you project so be conscious of what you are sending out as is possible. Work to get it right. Identify what you truly want and express it while eliminating the negative (no small task). Processing what you want becomes deeper than thought when you put it in writing. Sharing with others is perhaps the most powerful. The universe will take care of your requests. All you really have to do is have faith and believe. Attract the people you want in your life and business. Learn to get out of the way.

The spiritual law of attraction stated in another way says that "Whatever we hold in mind tends to manifest in our lives." This is an interpretation given to us by Dr. David R. Hawkins in many of his lectures and speeches around the world. It has also been expressed by Napoleon Hill. In general, it simply means that we tend to attract the things that we think about or focus on in our lives. By instilling our emotional energy into certain things, we call them toward us each day.

> "*Our minds become magnetized with the dominating thoughts we hold in our minds and these magnets attract to us the forces, the people, the circumstances of life which harmonize with the nature of our dominating thoughts.*
>
> *– NAPOLEON HILL*"

Keeping a positive attitude certainly isn't an easy thing to do. Each day, people will tell themselves many negative things. These negative ideas will sometimes be expressed in the light of day by a seemingly happy person and yet when we get to know the people who are thinking these ideas, we may find that they are actually quite depressed and afraid of many things. People make a lot of decisions based on these negative feelings and it isn't always apparent how much it is affecting their lives. It will often appear to be quite bad when you take a closer look inside. The negative tendencies that people pursue in their lives often help to confirm the initial fears that they have. They lose their jobs, their friends, and their closest loved ones to problems that seem beyond their control. This seems impossible e to change and yet, the law of attraction tells us something different. People's thoughts and decisions often promote the very kind of negative evidence that they initially set out to prove. They are the very cause of their own problems! The negative ideas that people project often function in a similar manner as a "self-fulfilling prophecy". By focusing on the negative, the negative comes to pass. The law of attraction tells us that, whatever we give our attention to becomes our point of attraction. It becomes the thing that we magnetize into our lives. This is even true for the things we try to separate ourselves from or fight against because we find that we are still giving these "negative" things our constant attention.

Let's look at an example. Someone decides that the worst thing in the world would be for their loved one to leave them. They worry about this day and night. It is their worst fear and they can't get it out of their mind. As they focus on this fear, they find that they simply cannot trust the person they are with. They are constantly second-guessing this person and accusing them of the fears they hold inside. Instead of showing them love and affection, they are actually driving this person away.

> "*When we create something, we always create it first in a thought form. If we are basically positive in attitude, expecting and envisioning pleasure,*

satisfaction and happiness, we will attract and create people, situations, and events which conform to our positive expectations.
– SHAKTI GAWAIN"

Blanco

OPPOSITE SEEMS TO ATTRACT

You've heard this said a million times and it certainly seems to be true in many cases. Opposites seem to attract. Oftentimes, couples seem as though they were two very different people. One is active, one is passive. One is cool and one is hot. Although these differences seem to exist on the surface, couples that stay together also have something more and this underlying vibration is the real thing that makes the attraction so powerful. People seem to be attracted to the qualities in another person that make them different. This is the way it appears on the surface and yet, this isn't the truth. As time goes on, the differences that seemed to attract these people no longer have the initial appeal that they first had.

Couples who are mainly focused on the differences that we have with each other, tend to argue and even despise those same qualities that seemed so great in the beginning. They often find that they have nothing in common after they have been together for a little while. In this case, they may start to realize that they need some similarities in order to balance things out.

Yin and yang tend to attract each other to create a balance but it is the underlying "balance" or "wholeness" that is really so attractive to these individuals. It is not the qualities of yin or yang themselves. An underlying vibration is necessary in order to keep those opposites together. The essential quality that is necessary to keep people together is often thought to be this wider vision of 'love' or 'peace'. Without this underlying power, the universe and the relationship would fly apart just like both Newton and Einstein might have helped us predict.

Although it may be true that opposites seem to attract, it is an even greater truth that opposites are only kept together by an underlying vibration of love. This power of love is an even greater power of attraction that supersedes the powers of yin and yang and becomes, for many people, the supreme power of attraction in the universe.

THE VOID

Another challenging idea along the path to creating our own destiny involves the idea of the void. This is an idea that originates in the idea of separation and can be seen as a way of looking at life or at the universe. In simple terms, the void can best be understood in terms of the things that we WANT and the things that we DON'T WANT. If there is a thing that we DON'T WANT, we focus on it wherever we go and divide up our experiences in relation to this hidden idea of emptiness or "negation". The "void" is an idea that has been presented to many spiritual seekers along their path and this is actually a form of negative thinking that is very subtle and insidious to the advanced seeker. We all give power to our hidden negativities and they take on a larger and larger context as we develop. This context, when it reaches its widest conception, is something that eventually manifests as the "void". If we can look more closely at this idea and try to uncover the negativity in our own thinking, it may help us to open it into a wider context of awareness. This wider context would, by its very nature, be a more attractive context simply because of the larger awareness that it allows.

First, let's look at an example. Some people are always dreading the future. They imagine that they will eventually have problems with their health or with their finances. They are always worried about what will happen to them down the road. After worrying about these outcomes, they find that they are very tired and need to take a break from the draining problems in their life. They decide to take a break from work because they are beginning to feel sick. They may stay home or even decide to quit their jobs because they "just can't take it anymore". "I hate my job" is one of the most common ideas that people tell themselves. "My relationships never work" is another common negation. With this kind of thinking, the future always seems to arrive with extreme predictability.

Inevitably, negative people tend to be viewed by others as lazy or irresponsible. People don't want a negative person working at their company or hanging around their circle of friends. These people often lose their jobs and find themselves incapable of paying their bills after their relationships go sour. They are often abandoned by their mates and can even enter into a severe form of depression. Oftentimes, they will even develop health problems and find that all of their original predictions about the doom and gloom of the world have come true.

People who see a negative future become discontented. This seems obvious and yet, negative people seem intensely committed to their own negativity. It is as though they felt there was some great honor in seeing the bad side of things. The evidence they were looking for about the world and the negative "reality" of life always seems to arrive with predictable accuracy because the law of attraction is working in all areas of the universe. In order to stop this negative thinking, it is best to look at the way it manifests itself so as to uncover a larger field of attraction and open ourselves to more positive energies.

RUNNING FROM FEAR

If we decide to focus on fear and grief, we will surely attract these kinds of things into our lives and feel a certain perverted satisfaction that our vision of negativity was initially correct. Even when we run from these fears, we cannot escape them. Running from fear only instills energy into our lives and helps it to manifest as a reality. Running from fear is not the way to alleviate this negative emotion. In fact, battling with any kind of negative emotion is only another way of attracting it into our lives.

If you have ever seen a person who is suffering from a mental illness, they can often be seen muttering to themselves or carrying on in a very strange manner. They may have acquired a sickness that paralyzes them in their lives. They will engage others with senseless arguments in order to satisfy their own sense of frustration or grief. What is so interesting is that others, who are less disturbed, will sometimes engage these people in elaborate discussions possibly in the hope of curing them or changing their minds. Quite often, the efforts are fruitless and only make the sane person appear worse off than when they began.

When a sick person and a good person get together, it is more likely that the two will both end up sick rather than the two of them both becoming well. Engaging in a battle over negative ideas is likely to only produce more negative ideas so that nothing is solved. This same idea holds true when it comes to fear. Engaging our fear as though it were something we should be afraid of is not the correct course. Instead of running from the things we fear or fighting against the things we dislike, we might choose instead not to waste our energy. We might take the high road instead and choose not to give in to the secret attraction that these arguments may have. We might turn the other cheek and look for something more positive to pursue.

Running from fear is only a way of expressing our own belief in the very power of fear. FDR's famous quote "We have nothing to fear but fear itself" profoundly suggests that fear is an empty idea with no power in and of itself. As long as we don't feed these fears, they will have nothing to live on and will eventually dissolve in the light of our own awareness. The law of attraction teaches us that this kind of positive thinking will only build on itself as we apply it in our lives. We begin to find that our courage is growing at enormous rates each day and the things we thought we should fear were only figments of our own imagination.

ACCEPTING OUR GRIEF

Depression is similar energy to fear but it is also a very common and natural phase of a person's development. As we learn to incorporate the negative ideas that we encounter in life, we also learn to reach for a larger context in which to understand these negative emotions. This larger context may eventually lead to a healthier attitude but this certainly doesn't happen overnight. As we begin to identify our negative emotions, fear and grief will begin to dissolve. The outside will eventually conform to our inner vision of things as we put the law of attraction into action.

It takes a lot of practice to overcome sadness and grief in our everyday lives and sometimes these emotions can go on for years. Oftentimes, people will turn to anti-depressant medication as a way of helping them get over these negative emotions. Anti-depressants can be very helpful in learning how to turn away from negative ideas and emotions and to incorporate more positive habits into our lives. Experiencing grief or depression can be seen as a positive step toward spiritual growth even if we need to turn to some help from science and medicine. We eventually discover that we were the inventors of those fears and that there wasn't any real basis for them in the first place. Looking at our own depression and sadness is a necessary phase of development and can be viewed in a positive light if we allow ourselves the chance to grow. The true reality in the universe is love but coming to this awareness is often a very long and arduous process. Eventually, we find the strength to view our grief as a temporary illusion that can also be dissolved in the light of consciousness.

> "*The opposite of love is fear, but what is all-encompassing can have no opposite.*"

– A COURSE IN MIRACLES

Many of our negative impressions come from an underlying belief that everything is useless, empty, and essentially a large void. People often talk about a sense of emptiness in their lives and avoid in their hearts that simply cannot be filled no matter what they do. If this void were truly the ultimate reality of the universe, then there would certainly be a good reason to assume that everything was ultimately negative. This, however, is simply not the case as both science and spirituality have come to show us. The one simple understanding that someone can have about "nothingness" is that by its own very definition it is "Not".

POSITIVE REFLECTIONS ON THE VOID

According to the great masters and many of the more modern interpretations of science, anything that can be perceived or thought of is always considered to be subjective in some sense. This is why the law of attraction works so well in our lives. Ideas about "nothingness" or the "void" do not have any real existence apart from a person's subjective experience. We are the ultimate creators of our own reality and coming to this realization is the only thing we need to do before our own happiness can become a priority. We eventually learn that there could never be a "void" if there were not someone like us to experience it in the first place. The observer, our Self, is the subjective reality that becomes the very proof that the "void" does not exist. We become our own proof of the reality of the world around us. This has been the natural progression of many great mystics over time, many of whom have experienced deep periods of depression or what is often called 'The Dark Night of the Soul.

> *"I could feel myself being sucked into a void. It felt as though the void was inside myself rather than outside. Suddenly, there was no more fear, and I let myself fall into that void. I have no recollection of what happened after that. I was awakened by the chirping of a bird outside the window. I had never heard such a sound before.....Tears came into my eyes.....I recognized the room, and yet I knew that I had never truly seen it before...For the next*

five months, I lived in a state of uninterrupted deep peace and bliss."

RELATIONSHIPS

Relationships are often what inspire us each morning to get out of bed and make an effort to improve our lives. The power of attraction is never more obvious than in the case of two people in love. This power makes each of us more eager and willing to make that extra effort in our lives and to go on with each successive day. The power in a relationship is also the thing that fuels people's sense of spiritual effort in their lives and gives them a sense of gratitude for their life.

ROMANCE

Romance is one of the most powerful energies that inspire an interest in spiritual life. It is the romantic ideal that is so intimately tied to our experience of love and ultimately to the greater meaning behind life.

"*– how fortunate are you and I, whose home is timelessness: we who have wandered down from fragrant mountains of eternal now to frolic in such mysteries as birth and death a day(or maybe even less) – E.E. CUMMINGS*"

Some of the most romantic ideas have been expressed to us through art and poetry and these fields are especially disposed to inspire a greater vision of what is sacred and most important to us in our lives. Romance is also closely associated with love as it helps to express the challenges that are encountered when two people strive to have a loving relationship. Love is always fraught with challenges and romance helps us to express these challenges in a more positive light.

One of the more widely held beliefs about romantic love is that there is often a mere ‘randomness’ to the encounter which eventually can be seen to have a wider significance in the more meaningful pattern of love. Romantic love is also commonly thought to involve an overcoming of obstacles in which the larger pattern is somehow threatened by a less meaningful element. Romantic love cannot be controlled and is therefore thought to be something beyond the individuals themselves.

The pattern of romantic love initially emerged in the Middle Ages when it was often the case that insurmountable barriers would separate two would-be lovers from their true destiny of eternal union. This is the typical image that we have when we think of romantic visions. The overcoming of age-old barriers often results in strong regard for ‘winning the love’ of the other person and it has motivated great efforts to be expressed through poetry, songs, and heroic battles since the earliest ages. Even today, writers go to great efforts to express this ongoing struggle and to revive the old passions of the earlier romantic ideal. We strive to express these ideas in the same way that we always have because the themes are always the same and will never change.

"We think, sometimes, there's not a dragon left. Not one brave night, not a single princess gliding Through secret forests, enchanting deer and Butterflies with her smile...... What a pleasure to be wrong. Princesses, knights, enchantments and dragons, mystery and adventure .....not only are they here-and-now, they're all that ever lived on earth!

– RICHARD BACH"

In our modern age, romantic love is still the theme of many forms of art and entertainment. Popular culture, as it is expressed through films and music is rich with romantic love. While romantic love is still the dream of many, some claim that the more modern presentations of the media are still not realistic. Romantic love, as depicted in books and movies, is thought to be extremely rare and may not even occur at all. Critics point at the modern dating practices in which sex is really the only true goal of the partners and a lasting relationship is almost never the case. Many people also suggest that the rigorous demands of money and careers often rob people of the romantic ideal and that the wider vision of love can never be realized.

MODERN DAY DRAGONS

Modern statistics and the many observations of psychologists also paint a somewhat dim picture about romantic love. Although love is certainly thought to be a reality that is possible in our age, it is often represented in the mass media as something other than realistic. The dragons of the modern age may still be alive and well but their imaginary quality may now come to us in a completely different way. Many argue that the modern-day dragons are intimately connected to the mass media in the way that it presents love as a romantic fantasy rather than a higher level of spiritual awareness.

"*Love as depicted in the mass media is not what this level is about. What the world generally refers to as 'love' is an intense emotional condition, combining physical attraction, possessiveness, control, addiction, eroticism and novelty. It's usually fragile and fluctuating, waxing and waning with varying conditions.*

– HAWKINS"

It may certainly be that love is still a realistic goal to obtain in our lives but many of the false ideas about romantic love may have to first be addressed if we are to overcome its obstacles in the modern age. We may need a new way of looking at romantic love that will help us to find our true destiny and a lasting relationship. Hidden underneath the temporary attractiveness of the common romantic notions will hopefully lie attention to our own spiritual practices and a more serious concern for the law of attraction.

GROWTH IN RELATIONSHIPS

As the attraction to the higher levels of awareness intensifies in our lives, an underlying vibration will become the glue that holds a relationship together. Attraction becomes more than just a temporary relationship between two people but rather a balancing force that continues to make each partner attractive to the other. The individuals move out into the world and begin to establish relationships in their careers and social lives so that they learn to practice the principles of love with everyone they meet. This is a further advancement in awareness that could be understood as the tendency toward unconditional love.

Love is often considered to be a power that can endure for eternity because it strives toward unity between all things rather than just two people. This eternal nature is also a tendency toward unconditional love as it incorporates not only the two individuals who were first attracted to each other but others whom they meet after they have first fallen in love. Growing couples learn to share their love with the others around them and move forward toward a more eternal vision of love. The tendency toward unconditional love may begin when a couple decides to move forward as individuals, either in their careers or in the case of a family.

FAMILY

Starting a family has always been the natural progression that a couple in love will embark upon. Just like the challenges they first face in their romantic love, the challenges they face with children are often profoundly underestimated. A mother and father must endure many more responsibilities than they ever imagined and arguments over how to raise the children are often at the top of the list when it comes to disagreements between spouses. The law of attraction applies here just as it has applied in every circumstance before. We become what we think about as individuals and as a family.

It is interesting to see the way children often take on very different roles from their parents. They have minds of their own and there really is no way of controlling them. In the same way that couples tend to create a balance between them, families also tend to move toward a balance and various roles will come into play so as to carry on this underlying vibration of wholeness and totality in the family. It is important to remember that we can only control the small things but not the big things. Family members will all have different visions of what is right for them and we must be open to the individual differences of each person. If the parents are to continue to strive for the higher level of awareness that they reached in their own relationship, they will have to continue to apply this to their children who eventually introduce new challenges to the family dynamic. It seems as though the original idea that opposites attract would be showing its colors once again and yet a family will not stay together unless there is an underlying set of values that hold the entire unit together.

Family patterns and family structure have changed a lot in the past few decades. However, it is still a great advantage for children if they are encouraged to pursue positive and worthwhile values in their everyday lives. Some of the more basic core values that help to promote a positive attractiveness are the pursuit of personal development, independence and responsibility, leadership, citizenship, respect for others, and a positive enjoyment of life.

In the case of personal development, children should be encouraged to develop physically, emotionally, and mentally. They should learn positive values that are related to their health, learning, creativity, and exploration. These may include the ability to trust themselves and others through the use of open communication and genuine concern. The healthy competition that springs from mutual support can also be emphasized. These attractive values help to contribute to the positive development of any individual and they are essential to promoting a better quality of life. In terms of independence, a child should be provided with an individual sense of freedom but should also learn personal responsibility and self-control. Activities that allow them to act independently and responsibly will encourage an attractiveness toward these values in greater proportions over time. Parents should allow children to make mistakes and then to learn from those mistakes. The children can learn to become involved in the planning and execution of their own future in a manner that promotes their own independence and personal responsibility.

Leadership is also an important value to promote in the family as it is closely tied to independence and responsibility. Many experts believe that leadership qualities emerge naturally as long as parents promote the values of being positive and enjoying the many opportunities that life has to offer. Parents can reinforce these ideas, however, by modeling the more positive and constructive values in their own families.

Citizenship is a higher-level value that children can benefit from as it helps them to recognize the value of the democratic process and their own role as a citizen in a democracy. Parents should recognize that their opinions, ideas, and values will strongly affect the perceptions of their children and eventually affect their overall attitude about their own careers and work ethic in the larger community.

Learning to respect others is probably one of the most important values that children can benefit from as it teaches them how to become attractive and to ultimately love another person. Respect is intimately connected to responsibility. Our responsibility to each other is what makes our relationships both lasting and loving. Children can learn that it is their own responsibility to see their behavior as having an impact upon others in either a positive or negative way and this will teach them to develop better relationships.

Finally, a positive enjoyment of life is probably the most central value that a child can learn. Life can be seen as great! It can have adventures, surprises and lots of joy.

Eventually, they may become leaders who inspire others by the way they perceive life. Problems can be seen as challenges to be overcome and as positive learning experiences rather than permanent obstacles.

By incorporating the many values already mentioned and others such as courtesy, acceptance, compassion and integrity, a family will become an attractive field of spiritual values where the members can thrive and grow. The law of attraction can be implemented in a positive way for both individuals and families so as to bring about a healthy manner of living.

HEALTH

Applying the law of attraction to our physical bodies is probably one of the most common applications that people use. We commonly think of attraction as something that has to do with personal appearance and we associate a healthy body with an attractive person. Maintaining our health will certainly make us more attractive and will also promote more positive thoughts and emotions. A healthy body leads to a healthy state of mind and maintaining these two things is all part of a positive spiritual approach.

NUTRITION

Nutrition is one of the most important elements of maintaining a strong body. A positive attitude toward nutrition will attract more information into your life about better and easier diets so that eventually your daily eating habits will become effortless. It is extremely important to have a good diet that will ensure the proper ratio of macro and micronutrients in the daily regimen. This nutritional concern will aid the body in its recovery process after a strenuous exercise and also maintain a general level of health and well-being. Adhering to a low-intake diet takes a lot of the stress off the body's internal functions and makes it a lot easier to maintain a healthy weight over time. This is just another example of the law of attraction taking effect in our lives.

EXERCISE

Physical exercise is also one of the most highly recommended ways of achieving good overall health in the body. This can be focused on various athletic abilities or just regular physical exercise. Whichever method we choose, it is proven that physical exercise is paramount in the prevention of many diseases such as cancer, diabetes, cardiovascular disease, and obesity.

Exercises can be divided into three groups; flexibility exercises, aerobic exercises, and anaerobic exercises. As we learn more about each form of exercise, we will also be presented with more opportunities to improve and widen our horizons in the exercise world. Flexibility exercises include the stretching of the muscles and joints to improve flexibility while aerobic exercises include walking, running, or swimming to increase cardiovascular endurance. Anaerobic exercises include more rigorous muscle exercises such as weight training or sprinting to increase the strength of the muscles. Physical exercise helps a person to maintain a healthy weight, healthy bones, muscles, and joints and promotes overall physiological and psychological well-being It also increases the strength of the immune system and may prevent the need for surgery or other invasive medical procedures down the road.

Exercise has been proven to aid in proper brain function by increasing the flow of blood and oxygen to the brain. It also increases the growth factor of nerve cells in the body by increasing the chemicals that are needed for cognition. The active breathing that takes place during exercise can help to increase a person's lung capacity and oxygen intake. This brings about greater cardiac efficiency because the heart will do less work when it has to oxygenate the muscles. Conscious deep breathing during aerobic exercise will help to develop heart and lung efficiency. All of these things work together to promote further advantages to our overall health and to give us even greater opportunity ies down the road.

YOGA

Yoga is a Sanskrit term meaning "union". It is an ancient spiritual practice that began in India thousands of years ago where it is still practiced as a great tradition. There are many forms of yoga such as Karma, Bhakti, Jnana, and Raja, but in the West, it has become more associated with various postures and fitness exercises which can eventually lead to a more advanced form of relaxation.

Yoga is a practice that certainly adheres to the law of attraction in that its advocates develop greater and greater expertise and eventually become attracted to the most advanced forms of yoga. These more advanced forms are practiced in the form of deep meditation and the ultimate experience of Samadhi or Enlightenment. It is said that the energies which an advanced student obtains from yoga will eventually and spontaneously attract the experience of Enlightenment through their own inherent powers and this is the ultimate goal of yoga. As a way of achieving Enlightenment, yoga is considered to be an essential part of both Hinduism and Buddhism and has also spread to many other religions around the world.

Traditional yogic techniques not only incorporate stretching and breathing exercises but typically include moral and ethical principles and a spiritual philosophy similar to that which is contained in the law of attraction itself. We call those energies toward ourselves which we meditate on every day and this is basically an advanced application of the law of attraction. Eventually, students may find themselves attracted to the specific teachings of a guru and may find themselves chanting specific mantras such as the sound "Om" which is considered by many enlightened masters to be the sacred sound of the universe.

Many people now see yoga as a daily practice that is beneficial because it leads to improved health, emotional balance, clarity of thought, and joy of life. Students of yoga may also be attracted to several breathing exercises and a stilling of the mind through the technique of meditation and this is merely a more focused aspect of the many yogic practices.

MEDITATION

Meditation is a specific element of yoga that generally involves the turning of a person's attention inward to the workings of their own mind and thoughts. It encompasses a lot of different spiritual practices but generally focuses on the mental activity and achievement of internal peace.

Many practitioners of meditation see it as a great way to become friendlier and healthier in their own lives. A derivative of meditation which is more commonly practiced in the Christian religion is that of contemplation where the mind is encouraged to reflect upon certain ideas so as to bring them into a more harmonious alignment with healthier attitudes and directions. An example of Christian contemplation might be the contemplation of the sufferings of Christ. Generally speaking, however, meditation tends to be a practice that focuses the mind on a single object or idea such as the breath or a sacred mantra. By practicing meditation, people become better at opening up to the powers of the divine and these powers become even more attractive as they develop inside each person.

CARRER

Once we begin to recognize that our old way of seeing things is attracting negative things into our lives, we begin to feel the attraction to become something else. We begin to focus on the things we love and this takes place in greater and greater intensity as we adopt a wider view of the world around us. We learn to accept things and to even experience gratitude for the way things are because this brings more joy and happiness to us. It is a difficult task at first as our old ways of seeing the world tend to permeate every area of our lives and negativity has become a very bad habit. It is even hard, in the beginning, to root out our negative emotions as their source tends to be very cunning and hidden from our view. In our work and at home we can especially see that we have established many bad habits that keep us stuck in the more narrow fields of consciousness and the magnetic power of these old ways is very hard to overcome.

"*The difficulty of inner work results from the great effort required to escape from the familiar gravity of lower attractor fields and move to the influence of a higher field. – HAWKINS*"

*I*n order to arrive at this higher level of consciousness, we eventually find that we must begin to apply a new awareness to every aspect of our lives. The spiritual effort becomes a daily practice that we apply to our careers and our relationships. At first, the efforts seem very difficult but eventually, we come to see that something else has been working in our lives which is far beyond our own personal power and has begun helping us along the way. In fact, this power has been there all along but we were not aware of its presence until now.

Our careers require extreme amounts of time and effort in our lives and yet, this area is often relegated to the 'back burner' when we think about spirituality. We think of our spiritual lives as a time to read or meditate and our careers as a time to make money and survive. Nothing could be further from the truth. Our careers are an intricate element of our spiritual lives and an area that needs considerable attention if we are going to attract positive energy into our lives. We will have to learn to think more positively about our careers if we are going to attract positive energy throughout our entire day.

A career involves more than just a job. A career involves a progression or an increase that brings us toward a greater level of success in our job. This happens by becoming more advanced in our spiritual pursuits. It is often a surprise to many people who practice a spirituality that some of the most successful career-minded individuals are also some of the most spiritual people in the world. It is the underlying drive to succeed that fuels people's desire to have a career and facing the daily challenges of a career is a great way to improve ourselves.

DESTRUCTIVE THINKING

Many people are dead set against money and careers. A common sentiment is that "money is the root of all evil" and many Americans believe that the corporations and the government are only out to exploit people for power and control. Money is often set in a bad light by those of us who may study spirituality or religion. The Eastern traditions often emphasize the importance of being "unattached" to wealth and success so that many people misunderstand the intentions of corporations or millionaires who are in possession of great wealth. Having a lot of money does not necessarily mean that there is going to be an attachment to money. Many great millionaires become philanthropists and help to solve enormous problems all over the world. It is the attitude that we carry toward wealth and power that creates the attachment that many religions often speak of. This is an idea which is very often misunderstood and which often leads to destructive thinking.

This misconception about the meaning of "attachment" often leads many people to think that you have to be poor and unemployed in order to be spiritual. A reverse sort of egotism can even set up with this kind of thinking where people will oftentimes see themselves to be 'better' than the rich and successful simply because they don't have any money or success themselves. As time goes on, these less fortunate people become unhappy in their lives because the rewards they imagined themselves to eventually gain for their commitment to poverty were somehow not materializing in the way they had hoped. They become angry at the world as if some mysterious enemy had taken over their lives and made them fall into a terrible misfortune. This problem only comes about as a result of people's negative thinking. They imagine a future when everything will fall apart for the rich and successful and they will get their just rewards. The future never arrives for having lived a life of poverty and unemployment and they wonder "What went wrong?"

The attachments of the ego take place in all areas of the world and not just for the rich and successful-minded people. A career can certainly become a place where people abuse their powers and exploit the less fortunate people of the world but it is also a place where the less fortunate can become bitter and resentful. The world around them simply becomes dark and hopeless because they never made the effort to overcome their unfortunate state. They hate the people in power and resent the larger order that has come to exist around them. Overcoming this kind of negative thinking is extremely hard. We have to start to consider the possibility that powerful people may only be doing their best to make the world a better place. We may not understand who the corrupt people are and who the philanthropists are until we have walked a mile in their shoes. A better place to focus our energies would be in our own lives and on our own negative thinking. In this way, we may learn to overcome these destructive thoughts and lead ourselves out of the negative patterns we have set up in our lives.

CONSTRUCTIVE THINKING

A career is a perfect place to set up your spiritual workshop because it is an area that requires a great deal of time and energy every day and involves almost every aspect of spiritual principles in order that you make it successful. Even if you are starting out at the very bottom as a dishwasher in a hot and dirty kitchen, you can make your career into an intensely spiritual pursuit that will eventually lead to other jobs and a more productive career that brings happiness and joy. Everyone needs a job of some kind in order to feel productive and the simplest or the most complex jobs are equally fertile ground for spiritual practices.

The key to long-term success is not in the particular job that you are doing. The key is in working on yourself as you do your particular job. This is constructive thinking because it makes it possible to use your time even more productively. When there is not an extremely important task immediately at hand, you can focus your mind on the present moment and simply experience your own inner consciousness. This effort will eventually widen the attractor field in which you find yourself and open up greater amounts of energy into your life. If you make sure and work harder on yourself than you do on your particular job, success will surely follow wherever you go. Once you begin dedicating hours a day to your personal development, your success will not be far behind.

EMERGENCE IN CAREER

In science, the concept of 'emergence' can be used to describe the way small jobs are ultimately related to their larger attractor fields. This concept of emergence helps to explain how these smaller, simpler tasks receive spiritual energy through their connection to the larger whole. This is the idea that more complex patterns arise from the more simple details of our behavior.

For an activity to be thought of as 'emergent' it is generally seen as unpredictable from a lower level. To the casual observer, it may appear as though the person is simply doing a very menial task that is unimportant. It is unpredictable and unprecedented, however, when the reasons for this simple behavior become more apparent in terms of a larger scheme. Although they cannot be explained by reference to typical explanations, a more complex explanation helps them to make sense.

In a typical job, a common reason for taking that job may be 'money' or 'opportunity for promotion'. These are common ideas that serve as simple reasons for going to work. They are fairly simplistic but are still commonly held to be the driving force behind many people's careers. If a person is doing the job in order to increase their spiritual connection, however, this may represent a new level in the system's evolution. This would be an example of an emergent pattern that could not be readily observable from simply looking at the individual person. It is a pattern that gives a greater significance to the person's job and would ultimately become more apparent as time went on because the person's career would begin to visibly reflect this hidden dimension. As the person's career progressed, the emergent pattern would be an extremely helpful and productive pattern of activity that could be seen more like a property of the collective whole rather than just a simple financial pattern.

In many cases, a person's behavior in their job cannot be explained according to lower-level reasoning. Many physical properties in nature are the same such as that of molecules that transmit sound. There aren't any specific qualities in the molecules which explain the larger pattern of behavior such as the transmission of sound. Emergent structures are patterns seen from a single event or a simple rule and yet they are still inherent in each individual part of the system. Although there is nothing that is immediately evident as an explanation for the behavior, the interactions of each part in relation to the larger whole lead to order and harmony that can be seen by each person.

MONEY

Money is one of the most common explanations that people use to describe the reasoning behind their job. It is an extremely simple explanation and yet it is often considered less than adequate to bring complete happiness in their lives. "I've got to pay the bills" is a simple yet insufficient reason for obtaining joy and harmony in our work. If we are to experience real happiness and a strong purpose in our jobs, we must typically involve ourselves more intimately with our job performance and make some kind of alternate contribution either to the larger purpose of the company or to ourselves. Money plays an important part in this sense but other factors such as improving our quality of life also play a role.

"*Successful people make money. It's not that people who make money become successful, but that successful people attract money. They bring success to what they do.*

– WAYNE DYER"

Donald Trump has expressed the importance of money in terms of "a scorecard that tells me I've won and by how much". Trump is one of the most successful real estate developers of the modern age. He is more associated with wealth and money than even Bill Gates, who is the richest man in the world. Donald Trump has explained that his happiness really doesn't come from the money but from the business dealings themselves. Trump obtains his joy in 'making the deal' and this only happens to generate large amounts of money as a byproduct. He certainly pays attention to the money but the real joy is located in the 'deal'. If Donald Trump couldn't make deals, he simply wouldn't be happy.

The pattern that emerges in the career of Donald Trump is one of many successful 'deal makers'. At first glance, people see money as the motivating factor because it is the simplest and most easy explanation. Of course, the money scorecard is definitely important but it isn't the whole picture. When we look closer, we see a more complex pattern emerging.

In other fields, money may also have a certain ability to serve as a scorecard but this scorecard may become less useful as we move into more subjective fields of work. Art, for example, is not always judged so well through its monetary value and yet, it can still be a very good way to make some initial judgments. In terms of money and our careers, we will always have to take into consideration the importance of this simple explanation but this is only an initial way of seeing the larger pattern in a career. As we begin to focus our spiritual efforts on our job and career, a larger pattern may eventually emerge which can bring even greater success.

GOAL SETTING

One of the most important elements to having a successful career is to think big. The more you are able to put into your mind, the better things you are going to achieve. Earl Nightengale has also said that a person's common problem is not that they can't achieve their goal, but that they never set the proper goals that they need to be successful. Setting the right goals is a very big part of achievement itself. A goal is sort of like having a dream that includes a specific deadline. The more detailed the goal is, the better. “Having a million dollars” is a great goal but it isn’t a very detailed one. A goal needs to explain the useful aspects that are going to assist you in your achievement.

Daily habits are a great way to fill out the details of a realistic goal. We have to make sure our work ethic will match with our dreams and ask ourselves if we are dedicated enough to carry through with the effort. The financial rewards are only one small part of a realistic goal. They will not typically work as a sole motivator in our career. Attention to spiritual values in our careers can bring about a more comprehensive practice which can then return to us as a worthy investment in the future. We will eventually learn to function in a productive way with the other people in our lives who will help to make us more successful as we move along our career path.

7 SIMPLE STEPS TO USE LAW OF ATTRACTION IN YOUR LIFE

Below are the 7 simple steps that you must follow in order to activate the Law of Attraction and manifest whatever you desire in your life.

1. DECIDE

The first step you need to do to use the Law of Attraction is to decide on what you want. You have to be crystal clear with your vision and the things that you want to be, do and have in your life.

Most people never go through this step and they wonder why the law did not work on them. It is just like goal setting, you must be crystal clear with what you want. Don't just say that you want to be rich or be happy.

These are vague requests and often, vague goals will produce vague results. Don't just say that you want to travel the world. You will end up going places that you don't want to. Therefore, be crystal clear with what you want.

Imagine you get into a cab and the driver asks you where you would like to go. What is your answer? If you say, "anywhere will do", guess what, the driver will chase you out or simply bring you anywhere. The same goes in life. If you have no idea what you want, life will throw anything at you.

And the same goes for the Law of Attraction. You must be clear with your request. Your desire is not clear, you will manifest whatever comes to you. The Universe will be confused with your request and thus, fail to give you the result you want.

Start by asking yourself questions such as what do you want to be, what experiences do you want to have, where do you want to live, and with who?

Your first step of deciding exactly what you want will become the fundamental of your manifestation. If your fundamental is blurry, you will not go far and your goals will never be realized.

Action Step:

Be absolutely clear with what you want. The more detail it is, the better. The message you send to the Universe will be clear and so it will be easier for you to manifest.

2. ASK

The second step you need to take is to ask for it. Once you have decided on what you want, you must then write it down and ask for it.

For instance, you can write down the car that you want to own on paper in present tense.

Here is an example:

"*I am so happy and satisfy now that I own a black BMW i5 and I'm driving it to work each day.*"

Don't ask in the future tense such as "I'm going to own a BMW i5". You must ask in the present tense as if you are living your goals.

Plus, use the word "I", because this word refers to yourself and it gives you a strong sense of ownership.

Besides that, remember to include emotional words such as "happy", "joyful", "satisfy", "thrill", "grateful", "enjoy", etc. These words are powerful because they bring out your emotions and make your asking process stronger and more realistic.

More importantly, you must be willing to ask for it daily. Make sure you refer to what you want every single day. It is just like practicing daily goal setting. Choose to write it down, review it, and think about it every single day.

The key is that you want to consciously turn what you want into your subconscious mind. You want to consciously program your goals, your dreams, and your wishes into your subconscious mind so that you can tap into the power of the Universe to manifest them.

Action Step:

Write down what you want and ask for them each day. You must consciously think about the things that you want to be, do, and have regularly so that you can program them into your subconscious.

3. Visualize

One of the most powerful steps that most people miss out while using the Law of Attraction is that they did not visualize what they want. And this is what you need to do in this step.

Do you know that visualization is a powerful technique that has been proven by science on its effectiveness in achieving what you want or improving your skills?

In 2006, a book was published and since then it has become a worldwide publishing phenomenon, translating into more than 50 languages, sold more than 20 million copies and has grossed over $300 million in sales by 2009.

Contents

The book is none other than the groundbreaking "The Secret". The Secret is a huge success and the content is based on one a powerful principle that everyone wants to learn, the Law of Attraction. The Secret popularizes the Law of Attraction and today, many people talk about it and want to know how to make it work.

And this is exactly what you are going to discover in this article. You will discover the 7 simple steps that you can use to activate the Law of Attraction in your life to achieve whatever you want.

The fundamental principle behind the Law of Attraction is that you will become what you think about most of the time. And thus, you can achieve your goals and materialize your dreams if you choose to consciously think about them on a regular basis.

Of course, this is only the fundamental. There is more than this if you want to make the law works in your life. Like the Aladdin lamp, once you have it with you, you can make your wishes come true, but you must know how to summon the genie to come forth.

The problem with most people is that they have no idea how to summon the genie. They have heard about the Aladdin lamp that can grant them any wish, but they have no idea how to use the magical lamp.

The same goes for the Law of Attraction. Most people understand what it is, but many did not know the real secret behind to make it work.

7 Simple Steps: How to Use the Law of Attraction in Life

Below are the 7 simple steps that you must follow in order to activate the Law of Attraction and manifest whatever you desire in your life.

1. Decide

The first step you need to do to use the Law of Attraction is to decide on what you want. You have to be crystal clear with your vision and the things that you want to be, do and have in your life.

Most people never go through this step and they wonder why the law did not work on them. It is just like goal setting, you must be crystal clear with what you want. Don't just say that you want to be rich or be happy.

These are vague requests and often, vague goals will produce vague results. Don't just say that you want to travel the world. You will end up going places that you don't want to. Therefore, be crystal clear with what you want.

Imagine you get into a cab and the driver asks you where you would like to go. What is your answer? If you say, "anywhere will do", guess what, the driver will chase you out or simply bring you anywhere. The same goes in life. If you have no idea what you want, life will throw anything at you.

And the same goes for the Law of Attraction. You must be clear with your request. Your desire is not clear, you will manifest whatever that comes to you. The Universe will be confused with your request and thus, fail to give you the result you want.

Start by asking yourself questions such as what do you want to be, what experiences do you want to have, where do you want to live and with who?

Your first step of deciding exactly what you want will become the fundamental of your manifestation. If your fundamental is blurry, you will not go far and your goals will never be realized.

Action Step:

Be absolutely clear with what you want. The more detail it is, the better. The message you send to the Universe will be clear and so it will be easier for you to manifest.

2. Ask

The second step you need to take is to ask for it. Once you have decided on what you want, you must then write it down and ask for it.

For instance, you can write down the car that you want to own on paper in present tense.

Here is an example:

I am so happy and satisfy now that I own a black BMW i5 and I'm driving it to work each day.

Don't ask in the future tense such as "I'm going to own a BMW i5". You must ask in the present tense as if you are living your goals.

Plus, use the word "I", because this word refers to yourself and it gives you a strong sense of ownership.

Besides that, remember to include emotional words such as “happy”, “joyful”, “satisfy”, “thrill”, “grateful”, “enjoy”, etc. These words are powerful because they bring out your emotions and make your asking process stronger and more realistic.

More importantly, you must be willing to ask for it daily. Make sure you refer to what you want every single day. It is just like practicing daily goal setting. Choose to write it down, review it, and think about it every single day.

The key is that you want to consciously turn what you want into your subconscious mind. You want to consciously program your goals, your dreams, and your wishes into your subconscious mind so that you can tap into the power of the Universe to manifest them.

Action Step:

Write down what you want and ask for them each day. You must consciously think about the things that you want to be, do, and have regularly so that you can program them into your subconscious.

3. Visualize

One of the most powerful steps that most people miss out on while using the Law of Attraction is that they did not visualize what they want. And this is what you need to do in this step.

Do you know that visualization is a powerful technique that has been proven by science on its effectiveness in achieving what you want or improving your skills?

In fact, many professional athletes use visualization to train and improve their skills to a higher level. This is simply because our brain cannot differentiate between what is real and what is imagined.

Thus, when you visualize, your brain will create new neural pathways and close the gap between what is happening in your physical world with your imagination.

John Assaraf, the famous guru who has been featured in The Secret is known for his story of manifesting his house through vision boards.

A vision board is a collection of pictures of what you want and it is used to help you visualize the achievement of your goals. Some people find it difficult to visualize the things that they want, and hence, a vision board can be helpful in this.

Furthermore, you don't just visualize the things that you want for once only and hope that the Universe will manifest them into your life. You have to practice visualization and do it on a regular basis.

It may be true that sometimes it is difficult to imagine the things that you are yet to own, especially in the beginning, and this is why you need to practice it often, preferably, on a daily basis.

Experts have shown that the best time to practice visualization is once in the morning after you wake up and once at night before you go to sleep.

Always remember this quote, "repetition is the mother of all skills". So don't just visualize once and then forget it. Do it on a daily basis. You can become good at visualization if you practice it enough.

And when you are good at visualizing the things that you want, the chances that the Law of Attraction will work for you will greatly increase.

Action Step:

Commit to visualization. Schedule a time each day to practice visualization. Choose a quiet place, sit down comfortably, close your eyes and imagine that you have already achieved all the goals you desire. Create a vision board to help you in this.

4. FEEL IT

Do you know why most people say that visualization and affirmation did not work? The main reason is that they did not include emotions into their practice when they visualize or affirm their goals.

You have to understand that emotion plays an important part in manifesting what you want and in the activation of the Law of Attraction.

If you are just visualizing the goals you want for the sake of doing the visualization, it will never work out for you. Don't just do it for the sake of doing it, you must include emotions and feelings into it.

Imagine that you are in a lecture hall listening to your lecturer giving his talk but he is not passionate at all. Do you think you will be interested to sit in the lecture hall for the passionless talk or do you think you will be able to absorb a lot from the lecturer? No, you will not.

Now imagine you are visiting a car showroom and all the salesman did is to read you all the information of the car from a brochure. Do you think you will be interested to buy the car? Not at all, even if you did buy the car, it is not because of the salesman, right?

The same works for the Law of Attraction. The Universe is listening to what you are saying all the time. Hence, if you are not persuasive, if you are not passionate, and if you are not putting in any feelings and emotions into what you desire, do you think the Universe will manifest them for you? You know the answer.

At a deeper level, thoughts are vibrations. And with emotions and feelings, you can send your thoughts to the Universe through a stronger and more powerful channel.

When you are visualizing what you want, make sure you add as many details as possible. See it as though it is real and is happening right now. Add in your five senses and feel the emotions.

Try to imagine vividly that you walk to your fridge, open the door, and you see a large yellow lemon in there. You reach out to the lemon and take it with your hand. Feel the texture. Now, imagine vivid that you take the lemon to your kitchen, and you use a knife and cut it into halves. See the juices oozing and now, take one piece of the lemon, squeeze the juice into your mouth. How do you feel?

Do you feel you have more saliva in your mouth right now? Well, if you imagine it vividly with all the details and you include your senses, your mouth will produce more saliva.

The reason is that your mind will think that your imagination is real and react to it. This is why you must include feelings and emotions into your visualization and affirmations.

Action Steps:

Every time when you practice visualization or affirmation, make sure you include your emotions and feelings into it. See the picture as real as possible and feel it with your senses. The more emotion you associate with your visualization, the more powerful and effective it will be.

5. GRATITUDE

Another important key step most people miss out on is gratitude. The majority of people are so busy in visualizing their dreams and making lists for their goals that they forget about gratitude, which is a crucial key to making the Law of Attraction work.

Gratitude is important in manifesting what you want in life because it raises your vibration and brings you into harmony with the Universe. In fact, gratitude is so powerful that it can change and transform your life.

To make it simple to understand, when you are grateful for everything that is happening to you, you will live better, you will feel that you have enough, you will feel loved, happy, and fulfilled. In other words, you are operating from a life of abundance.

On the other hand, if you are not grateful for everything that is happening to you, you will complain, you feel that everything is wrong, you struggle to pay your bills, you feel that your spouse cheats on you, and everything is not going right. You are operating from a life of lack.

Gratitude creates a life of abundance while complaining creates a life of scarcity.

Can you see now why the attitude of gratitude is important in your life right now? And because your thinking will create the vibration energy, so if you are thinking negatively, complaining and blaming all the time, your thought energy will not be in coherence with the Universe.

Meanwhile, when you are grateful, when you are feeling happy, and you appreciate all that you have right now, you are transmitting positive energy to the Universe.

Anthony Robbins once asked John Templeton what is the secret to wealth. Guess what Sir Templeton answered? He answered Tony, "You know it. You teach it, it's gratitude".

And here is the explanation from Sir Templeton, the investment pioneer who turned $10,000 into billions during the World War 2 era:

"Because if you have a billion dollars, and every day you live pissed off and frustrated, the quality of your life is called pissed off and frustrated. But if you have next to nothing, and are grateful for whatever it is you have, you're the richest person that you're going to know. It doesn't matter how much money you've got if you don't have gratitude."

So make sure you are grateful for everything that you already manifested and what you are about to receive.

When you are grateful for the things that you want, it shows that you confirm to the Universe that they are already yours and that you are open to receiving them.

Action Steps:

Here is what you can do to live your life with gratitude. Every day, practice writing a gratitude list. Write down everything that you are grateful for. It can be your car, your dog, your cat, your children, your wife, your job, your boss, your house, your computer, etc, anything you can think of and be grateful for.

Use the word, "thank you" more often and express your appreciation to everything that is happening in your life. More importantly, feel the emotion of thankfulness and gratefulness.

Take Action on Your Dreams

One of the core reasons people fail to achieve what they want through the Law of Attraction is that they don't do anything besides thinking about it.

If you only choose to think about what you want, you will never manifest what you want. Law of Attraction is more than just thinking. Money will not fall from the sky and your dreams will not come true without action.
Action is the link bridge between your dreams and your reality. If you want to bring forth what you want from your dreams, you must connect your reality with your dreams, through action.

Therefore, take massive and consistent action to accomplish your goals and achieve your dreams. Do something, work on what you want, and always be on the move.

5. TRUST AND BELIEVE

This step is where the magic happens. In order to activate the Law of Attraction and to make it work, you must trust and believe wholeheartedly for what you have asked for. Sincerely trust and believe that it will happen.

Most people fail with the attraction process because they don't believe that they can manifest what they want. They imagine that they become a millionaire and earn a huge amount of money, but deep down, they don't believe that it is going to happen to them.

When you do not believe that things are possible, you are sabotaging yourself in your mind. Your thoughts and not in alignment with your action. What you think and what you do will not be in coherence.

Take buying the lottery as an example. If you do not believe that you stand a chance to win, you will never buy the lottery ticket. You don't even bother about it. However, if you truly believe that there is a chance that you can win, you will go ahead and buy a lottery ticket.

Your committed action will show whether you believe it or not. If you believe that you cannot fail, you will do whatever it takes because you know that whatever you do, you will succeed. Conversely, if you do not believe that you can succeed and you believe that you will fail, you will never take action or try it.

This is why a lot of people fail to take action because they don't believe that things are possible in the first place.

They say that they want to be a millionaire and build a successful business, but you will never see they put in the effort and take action to make their dreams a reality. They simply do not believe that it is possible for them.

Successful people attract their dreams and achieve their goals because they are always in action. They believe that things are possible and that is why they take action.

To make it simple, you will never do it if you don't believe in it. Therefore, to use the Law of Attraction, you must believe that whatever you ask for is possible.

ACTION STEP:

Always do a self-reflection on what you do in life. Are you taking action or are you not? If you are not taking action, it shows that you don't believe that you can achieve what you desire in life.

Remember this quote, "You are what you do, not what you say you will do". Most people say and talk about their goals, but they don't include actions because, at the bottom of their heart, they don't believe they can achieve what they want.

7. RECEIVE

The final step you need to take is to receive. After going through all the steps, you must be ready to receive what you have asked for.

And sometimes in order to receive, you must let go. You can never start a new relationship if you still hold on to the old. If you want to buy a new car, sell off your old car. If you want to buy new clothes, get rid of your old clothes and make space for the new ones.

You can only start a new life when you clear off the old and make way for the new. Most people still hold on to their old beliefs, habits, mindset, and behaviors, and they wonder why the Universe is not bringing them what they want.

Imagine that you are a sponge and everything that is around you and happening to you is water. If a sponge is full, it cannot take in more water. If you are full, you cannot take in new things.

What you need to do then is to squeeze the sponge to let go release the water. And when you are empty again, you then allow yourself to take in and receive new things from your life.

Here is a very meaningful saying to illustrate the principle of letting go and be ready to receive:

"You cannot discover new oceans unless you have the courage to lose sight of the shore."

Therefore, be prepared and get ready to let go to receive what the Universe has in store for you.

ACTION STEPS:

There are many ways how you can practice this final step of receiving. One of them is through giving. Learn to give so that you can receive in your life.

If you want to thrive in your business, learn to create more value to your clients. If you want other people to treat you with care, be the first to care for others. If you want to be successful, solve other people's problems.

You can start from a simple act of kindness. Smile and greet strangers, hold the door for someone, buy food for the needy, and create more value to receive more in life.

CHAPTER FIVE

THE LAW OF CAUSE AND EFFECT

"Man becomes what he thinks about all day long. – Ralph Waldo Emerson"

The universal law of cause and effect states that for every effect there is a definite cause, likewise for every cause, there is a definite effect.

Your thoughts, behaviors, and actions create specific effects that manifest and create your life as you know it. If you are not happy with the effects you have created, then you must change the causes that created them in the first place...

"Change your actions, and you change your life... Transform your thoughts, and you will create a brand new destiny."

Our discussion today will focus on the immutable law of cause and effect and try to represent it in a way that will enable us to take advantage of its principles and use them to improve our lives. We will specifically discuss the premise that life isn't built upon accidents, chance or luck, while also looking at the dynamics of free choice — examining how we consciously and unconsciously choose what we experience and how we feel on a daily basis. To conclude our discussion we will list down several transformational analysis questions that can help us take advantage of this universal law.

The law of cause and effect states that:

> "*Every effect has a specific and predictable cause.*
>
> *Every cause or action has a specific and predictable effect.*"

This means that everything that we currently have in our lives is an effect that is a result of a specific cause.

These causes are the decisions we make and the actions we take on a daily basis. Whether our decisions seem small and rather insignificant, or whether they are significant and transformational in nature, does not matter. Each and every decision we have made and action we have taken has set events into motion creating predictable and specific effects that we are now experiencing in our lives.

This law of cause and effect further states that:

> "*Success in any field of endeavor is a direct result of specific causes and actions.*
>
> *Success in any field of endeavor is an indirect result of specific causes and actions.*"

This basically means that achieving success in any field of endeavor is predictable and can be repeated if we are aware of what we are doing. This essentially means that if you make the right decisions and take the right actions, you will undoubtedly achieve the success you envision for your life — whether you are directly aware of it or not.

As a consequence, the law of cause and effect brings to light the idea that success can be modeled once we are aware of what we want. All we must do is find out what successful people do, and we will be able to do what they do to achieve the success that they have attained in their own lives.

However, finding out what people do is only the beginning. We must also identify their:

- Decisions
- Habits
- Beliefs
- Values
- Emotions
- Meta-programs
- Psychological rules
- Behaviors
- Actions

What this essentially means is that we must intimately study these successful people from within their personal MasterMind Matrix. And only once we have identified how they are in all these areas, can we then take advantage of the law of cause and effect to help us attract similar results and success into our own lives.

There Are No Accidents

The law of cause and effect stipulates that:

> "*Success is not built upon chance or luck.*
> *Success is not determined outside of you.*
> *Success is created within you.*"

In short, the law states that there are no accidents in this world and that the effects we create in our lives are a direct result of causes that come from within ourselves.

The law of cause and effect goes on to say that:

> "*Everything happens for reasons, whether good or bad.*"

Because nothing happens by chance or luck, therefore everything happens for a reason as a direct result of the cause that you brought about from within yourself.

Whether good or bad, life doesn't play favorites. What you attract into your life is a direct result of the causes you brought forth into existence.

The law of cause and effect goes on to say that:

> "*Your life conditions create effects.*
> *Your life reactions to events and people determines how you feel and behave.*"

Who you've been, are today, and whom you're becoming tomorrow, is, in essence, creating the conditions and circumstances of your life and manifesting your future in front of your eyes. In fact, how you react to the events, people, and circumstances in your life is actually determined by how you feel on a daily basis — creating a chain of effects that are constantly transforming your destiny anew every day.

The law of cause and effect also discusses the power of our thoughts:

> "*Your thoughts create causes.*
>
> *Your thoughts give meaning to circumstances.*
>
> *Your thoughts are creatively manifesting your reality.*
>
> *Your life experience is a reflection of thought manifestations.*"

Within the seed of individual thoughts, lie the origins of the causes we create in our reality. These causes create effects which we experience in our lives as manifested life circumstances. In fact, our thoughts do more than just that. They actually give meaning to our experience of reality, which is why each of us holds a different perspective of the world around us.

You Have Always Had Free Choice

The one thing that is completely within our control from the moment we come into this world is our conscious power over our thought processes.

> "*The law of cause and effect states that:*
>
> *We choose how to interpret our experiences.*
>
> *We choose to experience emotions both consciously and unconsciously at any one moment in time.*

We choose to behave in accordance with how we think about the world, others, events and ourselves."

Because we have free choice to control our thought processes at all times, and since our thoughts create the causes that lead to the effects that we experience in our lives, then this, therefore, leads us to the conclusion that we have freely chosen to experience life as we know it, whether we are consciously aware of it or not.

The law of cause and effect further states that:

Free choice has created learned behaviors, responses, reactions, thoughts and interpretations of life and circumstances.

We are experiencing life as we know it because of the learned and conditioned psychological patterns we have pre-programmed into our minds over a lifetime of free choice. Moreover, this psychological programming is filtering our experience of reality in a very biased yet very predictable manner — effectively creating and interpreting our existence in front of our eyes.

The law of cause and effect does, however, provide a solution for this predicament. It states that:

"Because we have free choice, this means that we also have free choice to unlearn our thoughts, behaviors and reactions.

Because we have free choice, this means that we also have free choice to become proactive and conscious thinkers."

Free choice means that it is never too late to turn things around.

No matter how unfavorable our circumstances, how dark our predicaments or how unlucky we may have been. Free choice means that we can make a different choice and choose to unlearn what we have learned and learn what it will take to trigger the causes that will create the effects we desire to experience within our lives.

Transformation Analysis Questions

The law of cause and effect has provided us with several guiding principles that we can now use to create a set of transformational analysis questions that will help us to take advantage of this universal law instead of allowing the law to rule our behavior unconsciously.

The following transformational analysis questions will help you to gain greater clarity about your life and thought processes, allowing you to find the answers that will enable you to achieve the success you desire to experience in your life:

> *"How are my thoughts causing, creating and maintaining my current life circumstances?*
>
> *How can I begin interpreting my world differently?*
>
> *How can I change my patterns of thinking?*
>
> *How can I model other people's successful behaviors, habits, decisions, thoughts and actions?"*

Blanco

Concluding Thoughts

The principles behind the law of cause and effect are very deep and profound, allowing us to see life not as a set of random occurrences, but rather as a predictable formula of conscious free choice that can be molded and shaped to create the life we would like to experience and enjoy on a daily basis.

THE SIMULTANEITY OF CAUSE AND EFFECT

"“Choices made, whether bad or good, follow you forever and affect everyone in their path one way or another.”
— J.E.B. Spredemann, An Unforgivable Secret"

Buddhism teaches that the law of cause and effect underlies the workings of all phenomena. Positive thoughts, words, and actions create positive effects in the lives of individuals, leading to happiness. Negative thoughts, words, and actions on the other hand—those that in some way undermine the dignity of life—lead to unhappiness. This is the general principle of karma.

In Buddhist teachings other than the Lotus Sutra, Buddhist practice is understood as a gradual journey of transformation. This is a process in which, over the course of many lifetimes, the essentially flawed and imperfect common mortal gradually molds and transforms him- or herself into a state of perfection—Buddhahood. It is a process of self-perfection that requires painstaking efforts to accumulate positive causes while striving to extinguish the effects of past negative causes and avoiding new negative causes.

In Nichiren Buddhism, however, the attainment of Buddhahood is governed by a more profound principle of causality, as revealed in the Lotus Sutra.

AS WE ARE

The Lotus Sutra offers a radically different view of the human being and of the attainment of Buddhahood. In the perspective of the Lotus Sutra, delusion and enlightenment—the common mortal and the Buddha—are the two aspects, or possibilities, that are equally inherent within life, though life itself is in essence neutral. While the "default" human condition may be that of delusion, manifesting our Buddhahood does not require a fundamental change in our nature. In fact, the idea that Buddhahood is somehow remote from our ordinary reality is itself a delusion.

This difference between the pre-Lotus Sutra and Lotus Sutra views of enlightenment can also be explained with reference to the concept of the Ten Worlds. This concept describes our inner state of life at any moment in terms of ten "worlds," from hell to Buddhahood, which we move between constantly depending on how we direct our life and respond to our environment. In the pre-Lotus Sutra view, common mortals carry out Buddhist practice in the nine worlds (cause) and eventually attain Buddhahood (effect). The nine worlds disappear completely, replaced by the world of Buddhahood.

The Lotus Sutra, on the other hand, clarifies that

Buddhahood and the other nine worlds are each eternally inherent possibilities of life at each moment. Through faith and practice, the world of Buddhahood, which is otherwise dormant, is brought forth and the nine worlds retreat into a state of dormancy. This revolutionary perspective on "attaining" Buddhahood is expressed in the concept of the simultaneity of cause and effect. The nine worlds ("cause") and the world of Buddhahood ("effect") are in fact equally inherent potentialities existing simultaneously in our lives. The concept is symbolized by the lotus plant, which bears flowers (symbolizing the common mortal) and fruit (symbolizing Buddhahood) at the same time.

Here and Now

The difference between these two views of Buddhahood could be described using the analogy of a video game. The conventional view of the process of enlightenment is like a game character who gradually overcomes an array of inherent flaws, accumulating various powers and useful tools while successfully passing through to the advanced stages of the game.

In the Lotus Sutra's view of enlightenment, the game character is from the beginning already in possession of all the full powers possible and only requires a means to unlock them.

"The practice of Nichiren Buddhism is one of manifesting the potential of Buddhahood here and now."

Buddhahood here and now.

In real terms, this means that when we harness the inherent power of our Buddhahood, we can surmount any difficulty and establish a happy and victorious path of life. Furthermore, as the fundamental orientation of our life becomes one of hope and compassion, even our weaknesses and failings can function positively, becoming a source of understanding and thoughtfulness toward others. This does not mean, though, that we completely and finally transcend our capacity for delusion.

Bringing forth one's enlightened nature—characterized by courage, wisdom, compassion and life force—one is then equipped to engage fully with the problems of life, change reality for the better and make enlightenment an actuality.

Problems and challenges, in this sense, serve as a means for us to demonstrate the strength and reality of our enlightened nature and to inspire others to do the same. Buddhism is about living confidently and expansively here and now. The key component in this is faith in our inherently enlightened nature.

When we have full confidence in our Buddha nature and our ability to transform and triumph over any kind of suffering, problems become challenges to be welcomed rather than avoided. This sustained sense of confidence and determination in the face of difficulties is itself a manifestation of our Buddha nature and, in accordance with the principle of the simultaneity of cause and effect, assures our success in life.

CHAPTER SIX

THE LAW OF CORRESPONDENCE

> "*Our thought is the unseen magnet, ever attracting its correspondence in things seen and tangible. — Prentice Mulford*"

Law of Correspondence addresses the unique relationship between the Inner Self and the Outer Self - one being a reflection of the other; however, I'd like to take it one step further and suggest that there is a third essential component to consider when understanding how this Law works, and that is, the relationship with the Higher Self.

No doubt you're aware of the expressions, "As Above, So Below," or " On Earth, as it is in Heaven." Well, these ideas pertain to the line of communication, or correspondence, between the lower energies of the physical mind (Earth) and the higher energies of the Divine Mind (Heaven). The key to changing your physical reality is by realizing that you are more of a spiritual being than a physical one. Every step you take in your physical life reflects the spiritual self that is trying to be realized, which is why lessons are repeated in our lives over and over again until we learn them. When the transference of energy from our minds in the form of thoughts, emotions, actions, and words does not reflect a Higher Wisdom, this lower vibrational energy is, in essence, rejected and returned to us to revisit the same frequency until there is a match. This is why you can be overwhelmed with an emotion or situation you are dealing with. Instead of calling upon your Higher Self to assist in a resolution, your lower energies are being sent out and returned back to you saying, "Try again." This is a constant motion that occurs in each situation of our lives. The Law of Correspondence teaches us to acknowledge and look at an issue until it is healed. When one's ability to move through a challenge gets closer and closer to being aligned with Divine Wisdom, (by coming from a perspective of peace and love), then those negative, difficult types of situations will stop recurring in one's reality. This is when real change can occur.

AN ESSENTIAL DAILY GUIDE TO ACHIEVING THE GOOD LIFE

So how does understanding the Law of Correspondence shift our perception of the events that happen on the physical level? And how do we stay emotionally stable and wise in the midst of chaos? Let's investigate three ways in which we can make a conscious effort to align with the Higher Self and receive its guidance at times when the lower, physical self, is presented with unpleasant circumstances:

1. The Mirror Image

When you find yourself having a negative experience, recognize that somewhere there is disharmony in your inner world, and your outer world is reflecting that back to you. In other words, your Mirror Image is not of the True Self; it is of the damaged self. You are being shown the changes that need to be made and the places in your subconscious that need to be healed. When a negative emotion is triggered, it is important to take the time to understand why you are feeling a particular way and how you are reacting to it. Are you relating to your Higher Self or to your physical self? This is an important consideration because when you access your Divine Mind, the higher part of your existence, then you allow that mirror of your I Am Presence, which is Who You Truly Are, to be revealed within your physical body. So when you take time to change the negative inner thoughts and feelings into positive affirmations, that is when you are truly aligning with your Inner Truth. It is a moment in time in which you allow the true Spirit of You to become the Physical You.

2. The Opposing Force

Once you discover the lower frequencies happening in your outer world, you can transform them by applying opposite energy. Since our energy is reflected back to us at all times, know that when you are faced with something negative, the quickest way to dissipate that energy, heal your subconscious, and connect to your Higher Self, is to react in an opposite fashion:

When you are criticized, praise someone.
When you are hurt, love someone.
When you are discouraged, encourage someone.
When you are afraid, reassure someone.

In that moment, you are mastering the ability to heal a wounded part of you. You react from your soul's perspective, and thus, you recognize that We are One. Feed the energy that you desire, focus on good and positive thoughts, and the opportunity for healing is created.

3. The Flow of Life

Imagine yourself floating on a raft along a lazy river completely letting go and trusting in your safety. Each moment flows beautifully into the next. There isn't doubt or thought that something isn't right. To live one's life in peace and serenity is to live in harmony within the Law of Correspondence. However, when you encounter rough seas and are being tossed about, that is the wake-up call that your rocky outer world requires some fine-tuning by your inner world. The only lasting change that can take place is from within, then it will show up on the outside. Real change only comes from the Higher Mind (As Above) into the Lower Mind (So Below). Many think that changing the outside temporarily will result in a new, happier life, but they soon find out, hopefully, that the only permanent change comes from the Inner Self, which should accept guidance from the Higher Self. Try to flow with life as it happens, and when you feel a jolt, stop and ask yourself where the line of communication between your Divine Self and your physical self has broken down. More than likely, you will immediately see the discrepancy, and be better prepared and aligned next time.

It has become more and more important for each of us to be responsible for our own personal evolution and growth so that the world can be Heaven on Earth. But until that time, the fundamental challenge is being honest with yourself and realizing the potential you hold to create change on the inside and all around.

CHAPTER SEVEN

THE LAW OF COMPENSATION

"The Law of Compensation - Your income is determined by how many people you serve and how well you serve them."

"Compensation," wrote that each person is compensated in like manner for that which he or she has contributed. The Law of Compensation is another restatement of the Law of Sowing and Reaping. It says that you will always be compensated for your efforts and for your contribution, whatever it is, however much or however little.

Increase Your Value

This Law of Compensation also says that you can never be compensated in the long term for more than you put in. The income you earn today is your compensation for what you have done in the past. If you want to increase your compensation, you must increase the value of your contribution.

Fill Your Mind With Success

Your mental attitude, your feelings of happiness and satisfaction, are also the result of the things that you have put into your own mind. If you fill your own mind with thoughts, visions, and ideas of success, happiness, and optimism, you will be compensated by those positive experiences in your daily activities.

Do More Than You're Paid For

Another corollary of the Law of Sowing and Reaping is what is sometimes called the "Law of Overcompensation." This law says that great success comes from those who always make it a habit to put in more than they take out. They do more than they are paid for. They are always looking for opportunities to exceed expectations. And because they are always overcompensating, they are always being over-rewarded with the esteem of their employers and customers and with the financial rewards that go along with their personal success.

Provide the Causes, Enjoy The Effects

One of your main responsibilities in life is to align yourself and your activities with the Law of Cause and Effect (and its corollaries), accepting that it is an inexorable law that always works, whether anyone is looking or not. Your job is to institute the causes that are consistent with the effects that you want to enjoy in your life. When you do, you will realize and enjoy the rewards you desire.

Action Exercises

Here are two things you can do immediately to put these ideas into action.

First, remind yourself regularly that your rewards will always be in direct proportion to your service to others. How could you increase the value of your services to your customers today?

Second, look for ways to go the extra mile, to use the Law of Overcompensation in everything you do. This is the great secret of success.

Examples of the Law of Compensation

1. Here are some examples of how the Law of Compensation can work:
2. Give love and you will get love in return
3. Give happiness and you will get happiness in return
4. Go the extra mile and you may get rewarded in return
5. Spread your wealth and get more wealth in return
6. Think people are kind, people will be more kind to you
7. Think that money is abundant, you will get an abundance of money
8. Think that your life is worth living every second, your life will become magical
9. Be kind to others in your actions
10. Be kind to others in your words

CHAPTER EIGHT

THE LAW OF PERPETUAL TRANSMUTATION OF ENERGY

The law of perpetual transmutation of energy is rather complex. It is the reason pieces of thoughts become things. We are surrounded by energy, and it is always in motion. You might wonder what this law of perpetual transmutation of energy can mean for your rituals of manifestation and how does it work?

The Law Of Perpetual Transmutation Of Energy declares energy is constantly moving from one state of form into another in all things. This energy works to become something physical rather than staying in the ethereal realm. When you have a thought, idea, or emotional connection, this energy within your body is moving into physical form.

Understanding The Law Of Perpetual Transmutation Of Energy

This law is the basis of the idea of where thoughts transform into things. It may be a little challenging to grasp how a thought can result in something physical or something that can be experienced. Everything that we have created once started as a thought in our minds. Yet, it is a wondrous and beautiful miracle for everyone who lives in this universe.

Feelings and thoughts that are in abundance are trying to become real. It is something that you can eventually touch, use, and experience. When people create emotions, the perpetual Transmutation of Energy states that they must result in something physical and material. It is crucial to remember that regardless of the thought and feeling you may have, it will determine what you will attract.

For example, if you are constantly thinking of love and gratitude, it will create physical, real-world experiences of enhanced respect and appreciation. It is critical to stay consistent with the thoughts and intentions entering your mind since the universe will create circumstances that you have focused on.

When you waver or become inconsistent, it is challenging for the world to develop a solid matter from erratic energy. If you desire abundance but feel unworthy, you are sending mixed messages to your subconscious mind. Eventually, you will self-sabotage because you will always act according to what you believe subconsciously.

To create solid material out of energy, you will need to focus on the abundance in a positive perspective and realize that you are worthy. Eventually, your manifestation will be on its way to you. It creates constant energy for the universe when you perform this, which you can utilize to turn into real-world objects and experiences.

Regardless of whether it is positive or negative, energy is always manifesting in physical ways. It is helpful if you take the negative energy you are feeling and transform it into something positive. You can use different positive techniques to increase your positivity when it's low. For example, listening to positive affirmations, audiobooks or podcasts can boost your positivity and focus your mind on creating something better.

The Law Of Perpetual Transmutation Of Energy Works

We can use three primary methods to guide the law of perpetual Transmutation of energy within ourselves. Having control over your mind and actions is the best way to transform your outcomes and results. Without taking responsibility for our thoughts, emotions, feelings, beliefs, and actions, nothing in your world will change.

1. Actions: The most essential way to change your current results and begin to manifest your dream life is by taking the correct action every day. Without the appropriate efforts towards your primary purpose and goals, your energy won't manifest your vision. Therefore, the best way to transform your energy to receive what you desire is to take massive action on the goals every day.

2. Thought: Believe it or not, studies suggest we have around 80,000 thoughts daily, and 90% of them are repeated every day. If you don't remove the negative thoughts controlling your life, you can't expect a better mindset. It's essential you're conscious of negative controlling thoughts and remove and replace them with

positivity. If you continue to have negative thoughts of lack, fear, stress and worry, you're creating more of that energy.

3. Words: The words you use not only impact others but imprint onto your subconscious mind. If you use words of scarcity, inferiority, lack, and self-doubt, your subconscious mind accepts that's your reality. Your energy is vibrating low, and you attract those words into physical existence. Even if you haven't manifested your dream life yet, utilize words that only describe your future and never allow words to hold you back.

How To Apply Perpetual Transmutation Of Energy For Manifesting Abundance

Your subconscious is where every work of changing or transmuting thoughts into tangible reality occurs. To access the full potential of your subconscious mind, you must train it to align with your intentions. The same is applicable in manifesting money.

For instance, people often have conflicts that bother their minds. The conscious level of your mind might be focusing on building a massive business to manifest money. But your subconscious is doubting your ability to accomplish something extraordinary. These conflicts send mixed messages and energies to the universe, which can mitigate your progress.

Don't Allow Negativity To Decrease Your Energy

It would help if you accepted that a problem exists, and only you can solve it. The universal law of nonresistance states that once you are resisting, it will always persist. It connects to the law of karma as well as the law of change. It says that a situation might repeat itself until the lessons are learned. You might find numerous people stuck in negative experiences as they go about their routine because they pay considerable attention to negativity.

For example, if a person is paranoid about failing, it might limit them from trying new ideas. Keep in mind that when you invest considerable energy into resistance and do not allow certain things to occur, everything in your life will grind to a halt. But if you allow yourself to hope on the possibility of winning at what you are embarking on, the universe opens up its portals of energy. Thus, success flows through you.

Don't worry endlessly about problems. Instead, you must seek solutions. If you nurture a mindset that focuses on solving problems, it will result in the reality you want, no matter the hardship you face. It is best to discipline your mind and think positively. It would help if you tuned in to your thinking patterns.

Eradicate your tendency to dwell on themes such as fear, shame, or anything negative. Keep in mind that the response you provide to a situation is what will determine its outcome. Train yourself to respond rather than react, and you will have fewer problems.

Overcome The Limits Of The Ego And Control Your Energy

There are plenty of ways you can tell when your ego is mitigating you from allowing energy to flow through you and undergo Transmutation. If you constantly complain about every tiny thing that goes wrong in your life, you can be sure that your ego is controlling you.

The ego blocks you from seeing things in a positive light. It forms a disconnect between you and your surroundings. When people sense that you are inauthentic, they will distance themselves from you. Try to limit your overthinking. Keep in mind that when your ego is in control, you will find yourself suffering negative emotions.

CHAPTER NINE

THE LAW OF RELATIVITY

The Law of Relativity states that every single soul on this planet will face challenges from time to time. However, the degree of challenge is relative and nothing is ever as bad as it seems. This law reminds us to keep our perspective in check. Life is always happening for us and not to us, so judging our challenges only makes us feel less empowered to get through them. We must understand that any obstacles, challenges, or "problems" that we face were divinely planned for us to make ourselves stronger, better, and help us evolve into the best versions of ourselves.

Each person will receive a series of problems (Tests of Initiation/Lessons) for the purpose of strengthening the light within each of these tests/lessons to be a challenge and remain connected to our hearts when proceeding to solve the problems. This law also teaches us to compare our problems to others‘ problems in its proper perspective. No matter how bad we perceive our situation to be, there is always someone who is in a worse position. It's all relative.

The spiritual and metaphysical aspects of this law of

relativity tell us that everything in our physical world is only made real by its relationship or comparison to something. Light only exists because we compare it to dark. Good can only exist because we compare it to bad. Hot can only exist because we compare it to cold.

In fact, everything in our life just is until we compare it to something. Nothing in life has any meaning, except for the meaning that we give it. It is all in how you look at your situation and what thoughts and perspective you choose to think about the situation with. When you focus on good thoughts and energies, more good things will come to you. Likewise, if you focus on how bad your situation is, you will attract more bad.

You can always compare your life situation to someones else, and it will look better or worse depending on your viewpoint and how you look at it. If you compare your situation to someones whose is worse yours will look better. No matter the situation at hand, 'There is always someone worse off and there is always someone better'.

However, from a spiritual point of view, we can remove barriers of labeling and accept everything 'as is'. From A New Earth by Eckhart Tolle: "Inform, you are and will always be inferior to some, superior to others. In essence, you are neither inferior nor superior to anyone. True self-esteem and true humility arise out of that realization. In the eyes of the ego, self-esteem and humility are contradictory. In truth, they are one and the same."

CHAPTER TEN

THE LAW OF POLARITY

> *"Everything is Dual; everything has poles; everything has its pair of opposites; like and unlike are the same; opposites are identical in nature, but different in degree; extremes meet; all truths are but half-truths; all paradoxes may be reconciled."--The Kybalion"*

The Law of Polarity states that every single thing in this Universe has its polar opposite. Joy has sadness, light has dark, and up has down. Many get frustrated with the fact that polar opposites exist, but the Universe does this to serve us. We will get what we don't want in order to have even more clarity on what we do want, and actually appreciate it when we receive it. It's hard to truly be grateful for joy when we have never before felt sadness. It's hard to appreciate the beautiful sunlight when we've never experienced darkness. Polarity exists so that we can exercise our focus. Just like a muscle, focus requires persistent practice in order to strengthen it. By having polar opposites, we get really good at focusing on what we do want rather than what we don't want.

Every thought (and therefore every intention) has two components; CONTENT and ENERGY.

So, for example, when you want to manifest a new love, that raw information is the content of your intention.

Meanwhile, energy is the power that drives that intention. It's the energy component that is intimately bound up with the Law of Polarity, and this energy component is powerfully influenced by your subconscious.

According to the Law of Polarity, everything is dual. So things that appear to be opposites are actually two inseparable parts of the same thing. Think of hot and cold, for example; although they're opposites, they're actually on the same continuum and you cannot have one without the potential for the other. You can think of whatever you want to manifest in the same way. For example, abundance is inseparable from financial lack, love is inseparable from being alone, and success is inseparable from failure; each comes with the potential for its opposite.

So once you understand this concept, try writing down what you want to manifest, and write down its opposite. This is the start of applying the Law of Polarity effectively.

Failing To Manifest Through The Law Of Polarity?

The deep-seated negative beliefs in your subconscious (e.g. that you're not talented enough to succeed or attractive enough to fall in love) shape the energy of your intentions. So, even if you're thinking about the content of your intention, such as finding a great partner or earning an amazing job, your emotional energy may not be in tune with this intentional content.

(By the way, if you're not sure what your limiting beliefs are and what is holding you back, take this free test here and find out what is stopping you from using the Law Of Attraction effectively).

If you're experiencing strong emotions like excitement and joy in connection with your intentions, you have a strong intentional current that will help you manifest. If those emotions just aren't there or they're wildly inconsistent, you're lacking the right kind of intentional current.

Make a note of the emotions you experience in relation to your intentions. Consider whether they're associated with a strong intentional current or not.

A battery, with its polar opposite terminals; one positive, and one negative. If you hook it up to a circuit in one way, a current will be created by electron flow. However, if you hook the battery up to a circuit in the opposite way, the flow of electrons will reverse and the electrons will flow in an identical current in the opposite direction.

If you want to boost the current, any extra batteries you have need to be aligned to create a current in the same direction. If you add extra batteries and some of them are facing the wrong way, you'll disrupt the current and the device won't work.

In many cases, people working with the Law of Attraction don't have an effective energy flow because they're accidentally using both polarities at once. If you have both polarities present at the same time and in the same magnitude, they simply cancel each other out.

Even if you're pouring a lot of energy into your intentions, you're working against yourself if you're accidentally mixing polarities. And are unlikely to manifest the life you think you want.

Try to spend some time reflecting on whether this might be true for you.

Everything is on a continuum and has and opposite. We can suppress and transform undesirable thoughts by concentrating on the opposite pole. It is the law of mental vibrations. We can see that you cannot have a left without a right, an up without a down, failure and success, a good without a bad and so on, it is a world of duality. However, these opposites have no absolutes, there is not one point where you can say one starts and the other begins, it is a scale range.

There are two poles or opposites, the difference between the two extremes of one thing is called polarity.

There are degrees of difference between the extremes or poles no absolutes. This law states that, in fact, these opposites are simply different manifestations of the same thing! For example there is not one point where you can say that cold stops and heat begins, its all on the same pole.

Napoleon Hill, author of the classic Think and Grow Rich, wrote "*Every adversity, every failure and every heartache carries with it the seed of an equivalent or a greater benefit.*"

An understanding of the Principle will enable one to change his own Polarity, as well as that of others, if he will devote the time and study necessary to master the art.

Mastery of the Law of Polarity requires learning how to maintain balance, focus, and detachment from the distractions of the material world.

Everything has an opposite on the same continuum

How would you know what heat is if you didn't experience cold? How would you know the feeling of joy if you didn't ever feel sadness? You need one to experience the other, and this is the gist of polarity. So let's take a moment to be grateful for the 'bad' things in life that allow us to experience the good things. I live in a climate where we get cold, dreary winters. But I've learned that it's what makes the joy of spring such a wonderful experience, and what makes me love and appreciate the sun-filled, hot summer days even more.

> "*All truths are but half truths and every truth is half false, there are two sides to everything, opposites are identical in nature yet different in degree*
>
> *The Kybalion*"

We can apply the same concept to our emotions: through the despair of losing a loved one to illness, we can learn appreciate our own health, and not take for granted the time we have with your family and friends. Without sadness, how would we know what joy feels like? Without one, the other ceases to exist. All of our human emotions are part of the human experience and serve a greater purpose, whether they feel good or not.

CHAPTER ELEVEN

THE LAW OF RHYTHM

The Law of Rhythm reminds us that nature is seasonal and cyclical. Since we are innately a part of nature, we too have seasons and natural rhythms. We must only work when we feel inspired to put in the work and rest when we feel inspired to rest. Just like we can't expect 365 days of summer, we can't expect to be energized, happy, and productive every single day of the year. Winter comes around every year to give us a break; To nurture our souls, and to rejuvenate our spirits. This is also to say that we can't expect 365 days of winter either. Trust that the inspiration will come back once you've had your rest.

In "The Light Shall Set You Free," the Law of Rhythm states that everything vibrates and moves to certain rhythms. These rhythms establish our seasons, cycles, stages of development, and patterns. There is a time and a season for all things in the universe and beyond.

> "*"Everything flows out and in; everything has its tides; all things rise and fall; the pendulum swing manifests in everything; the measure of the swing*

> *to the right is the measure of the swing to the left; rhythm compensates [counterbalances]." – The Kybalion*"

There is no such thing as absolute rest in the universe. In everything, there is a manifested measured motion, an action, and a counteraction that has rhythm. It is manifest in everything from the creation and destruction of worlds to the rise and fall of nations, governments, movements, philosophies, creeds, fashions, living beings, their mental states and matter.

> "*"These rhythms constitute an order of renewal in the universe, that can be either disruptive or pleasant, depending upon how one wishes to perceive these rhythms." – Norma Milanovich & Shirley McCune ("The Light Shall Set You Free")*"

The Hermetic Masters understood that there are two planes of manifestation: lower and higher consciousness. Using the Law of Neutralization, they could escape the swing manifest on the lower plane by rising to the higher plane. They were able to let the negative moods, feelings or mental states pass beneath them without being carried along with them. They also held that:

For every high there shall be a low, and the negative is precedent to the positive. The lives are always counterbalanced, even though several lives may be required to do that.

When our lives are in balance, we experience the positive cycles and emotions of faith, generosity, kindness, patience, love, courage and duty.

When we experience the negative cycle, our feelings and mental states change to more fear, anger, envy, criticism, worry or blame. When we tire of the lows, our soul is more open to learning new ways to master its emotional and mental states and behaviors.

The key to mastering this law is to use the strength of our will to remain positive, to overcome or transmute the negative swings, to rise above or detach from them.

How do we do that?

We may think of rhythm in terms of "time," which doesn't exist outside of our 3D reality. All events are happening in event space or parallel conditions in the Now. Nora Herold explained:

We can unplug from linear time and see ourselves as existing in the Now. We are stepping away from stringing together our moments into a story with a beginning and an end.

We can operate as multidimensional beings, who understand that we are inventing and reinventing the entirety of our experience in each and every single moment.

We can see each moment of our experience in this life and all other lifetimes as simply "bubbles of information" floating in the space all around us.

In this visualization, suddenly there is no time. There is no past, no present, and no future, because they're all just event bubbles existing in the field around us. Then we can say:

> *"It's not what happened to me so long ago. It is just one moment in "time" that I have owned as my "past" that now I simply can see as an experience that my oversoul had, like all the other lifetimes."* –

Nora Herold"

Because these moments are just bubbles of experiences, they no longer have to define our current Now moment. We can choose to feel however we want to feel in this Now moment.

We don't have to pull the data from any moments that would take us to a lower place of victimhood, enslavement, powerlessness (e.g. childhood or past life trauma or disease).

The information is there for us to access and use, when it's for our highest good to use it. We just need to ask ourselves: How am I feeling? What do I need in this moment?

Herold said WE are recreating ourselves as new again and again and again. We don't need to tie ourselves to old stories (e.g. being rejected, sick). Let yourself play with the bigness of this!

What is meant by the flow?

In the I Ching system, there are several gates that relate to the Law of Rhythm, including the Gate of Beginnings (53), Gate of Continuity/Endurance (32), and Gate of Growth/Cycles (42). There is also the Channel of Rhythm composed of two different gates:

Gate 5 is called the Gate of Waiting or Fixed Rhythms. It's all about being in the Flow while having the power to fix individual patterns (e.g. daily routines, habits, rituals). Its Shadow state is Impatience (manifest as being pessimistic or pushy), which can move to Patience (Gift) and Timelessness (Siddhi) with increased awareness and mastery.

Gate 15 is the Gate of Extremes or Modesty (balancing the extremes). This gate is about embracing different rhythms and extremes of behavior in humans and in nature (e.g. animals, elementals). It goes from the Shadow of Dullness (being stoic or extremist) to Magnetism (Gift) and Florescence (Siddhi), drawing people into a continuous flow.

Gate 5 is fixed and disciplined, while Gate 15 is flexible and adaptable. They work together to bind all life forms into the universal rhythm. They magnetically pull other people into their flow, which can be positive (e.g. peace) or negative (e.g. genocide) in direction. We have the option to participate (or not) in any of the collective flow patterns or event streams around us.

Final Thoughts

The Law of Rhythm is played out on all levels of the multiverse. The multiverse itself oscillates through cycles of expansion and contraction within the Origin, just like the entities that are using the multiverse structure for their own progression at various universal levels.

This lifetime is happening at the same time as all our other lifetimes. They are being counter-balanced from a higher state of "timelessness" by our True Energetic Self (Oversoul/Higher Self) as needed for our growth and evolution. We just need to trust the process!

Rhythm is easy to see in nature. The hummingbird lives and vibrates at a completely different rate than the flower it lands on, but both live in cycles adapted to each other.

The Law of Rhythm describes how the flow of energy from the Sun reaches the Earth and describes how it reaches its center, is reversed by the collision, and returns back to the Sun. To know more about the law and how it works, we must think about the energy in the universe being like a pendulum. A pendulum swings to the right, but it doesn't stay there does it? No. It then swings back to the left. It keeps this rhythm back and forth, back and forth indefinitely. Everything in existence is involved in a dance... swaying, flowing, swinging back and forth. Everything is either growing or dying.

There are times when things seem out of rhythm because it makes you feel uncomfortable. Your job is to stay focused on your vision and go with the flow instead of resisting it. To get a better understanding of how Our task is to deal with these changes in the season responsibly. It is all in how we respond to these rhythms that make the difference. We can choose to accept them for what they are and ride the tide or we can fight against them. The choice is ours. Just remember if you choose to fight you will bring only more of it into your life. If you ride the tide of change you will soon be facing a new season.

The law of rhythm also governs our economy, health, relationships, and spirituality. Let's say that you're at peak potential with your health and fitness. If you realize you're at the peak, then you can foresee your health and fitness dropping some. However, instead of viewing this "drop-in health" as something being wrong with you, you now view it as a sign to rest your body. Then, by law, you have to grow to a better and higher state of potential. Masters know how to rise above negative parts of a cycle by never getting too excited or allowing negative things to penetrate their consciousness, the key to success in mastering this law is in balance. Never allow your emotions to swing too far to the left or right.

The law of rhythm can be considered as governing four actions: right or wrong rhythm in feelings, right or wrong rhythm in thinking, right or wrong rhythm in speaking, and right or wrong rhythm in acting. Not only hate but even love that is not maintained by rhythm will fail. Not only an evil thought but even a good thought will prove to be disastrous without regard for rhythm. Not only false but even true speech which has no rhythm will prove to be fatal. Not only wrong action but even right action devoid of rhythm will prove to be out of place. In order to maintain a perfect condition in life one must be the master of rhythm.

CHAPTER TWELVE

THE LAW GENDER

> *"Gender is in everything; everything has its Masculine and Feminine Principles; Gender manifests on all planes." — The Kybalion."*

This Law is evident throughout the whole of creation in the opposite sexes: in humans, in plants, in animals, in electrons, and even magnetic poles. It states that on all three planes, it is impossible for creation to take place without this Law.

On the physical plane, every person has a male or female physical body but psychologically, every person is androgenous with both female and male qualities.

The Law of Gender is the last of the Universal Laws I share.

Yin and Yang. There is both a male and female part of each of us inside.

The Law of Gender exists throughout all of nature. There isn't one place it isn't found.

We each have the divine masculine and the divine feminine inside.

It doesn't necessarily have to do with whether you're male or female in physical body.

If a male is more right-brained, he's coming from a more feminine side, which has nothing to do in this case with his sexuality.

As that part of him is encouraged, or exercised, the left side begins to atrophy, if the left side is not also exercised or encouraged.

The same happens with females.

As humans, we need to balance these sides so we bring in the feminine and masculine and embody both.

The most successful people in the world are able to go back and forth between the feminine and masculine sides of their personalities at will, without a problem.

They can relate to both sexes very well. It allows them to be successful, because not only do they have the creative side of them that is coming forward, which is the feminine side, they also have a focused willful side, which is the masculine side.

Eckhart Tolle in his book, A New Earth, speaks about how our planet has been more masculine for thousands of years and how we need to bring in the divine feminine to balance it. He states that because of this imbalance, ego has had supremacy in the human psyche.

We are all connected to God/Source/Spirit whether we are aware of it or not.

It's important to pay attention to who you're being.

Both men and women need to give themselves permission to be both sides, regardless of what anyone else may think.

It all comes down to loving ourselves. In order to do that, you really need to become aware of and love both sides.

A part of this Law is that there is a gestation period with creation most of the time. Yes, there can be instant manifestation, only the majority of the time, as in nature, there is a gestation period.

Plants and trees couldn't exist without their respective seeds. As it is in all of nature.

Faith and belief play a vital part as the gestation is occurring, to it's success.

It's easy to believe in something you can see happening, but true faith and belief, is to believe in the unseen.

As we live in this physical world, there is also a spiritual world.

When you create those new intentions for your life, you're drawing from the formless substance or the spiritual world. As I've talked about in the past, setting intentions daily, is vital for you to become a conscious creator of your own life.

Many people stop right before their manifestations occur.

As you lose momentum by having doubts, and not having faith, you slow down your manifestation process or it's lost.

Therefore many dreams you have are never realized because of your doubts.

The Law of Gender is a Law that can help you reinforce the belief that what you want in life is coming. What you are seeking is seeking you.

You must be completely open to receiving it, however!~

Understand that everything in this world has a yin and yang, male and female, and a gestation period. It's only a matter of time before your circumstances change. Keep the faith!~

The law of gender is easily one of the lesser-known of universal laws, but don't just ignore the law of gender. Like all the other laws, the laws of gender are important for a fulfilling life.

The law of gender is similar to the law of polarity; it is about opposites. Where the law of polarity is about opposites of anything and everything, the law of gender looks at 2 energies: Masculine and Feminine.

Everything in the world has masculine and feminine. Everything is masculine AND feminine.

The most commonly viewed and probably well-known way to look at this is the yin and the yang. The yin is the feminine energy and the yang is masculine. They both are intertwined, making a whole being. But look closely, within the feminine lies a small dot of masculine, and within the masculine lies a small dot of feminine, representing that both the masculine and feminine are present in the masculine and the feminine. It is in everything.

Why is the Law Of Gender important?

The law of gender is important because it shows both sides – the feminine and the masculine – of everything. And each has its own traits. If we can know that everything has masculine and feminine, and understand how to notice their traits, we can start using the law of gender to benefit our lives.

Feminine energy is very giving, receptive, passive, and inward flowing. It is our empathetic and compassionate side. The feminine energy is electrical. It's the ME – the self – in I AM.

Masculine energy is taking, action-oriented, and outward flowing. It is the power of will, determination, and conscious mind. It is the magnetic side. It is the I in I AM.

Everything in life presents itself with these 2 sides.

Right and left brain, for example. One side boasts logic (masculine) and the other side boasts creativity (feminine).

The soul and the ego are the same way. The soul is present, and calm (feminine) whereas the ego is dominant and forceful (masculine).

It is important when we discuss this that we do not get too convoluted in the discussion of gender, gender roles, and which gender someone is. This is not what this is about, and frankly, there is too much noise about that in the world today.

This is about energies, and understanding that everything, everyone has feminine and masculine energies, even males and females. Females possess masculine energies within them, although mostly feminine energies are dominant. The same goes for males on the flip side.

Understanding these energies, and that they are all around us, will help you to live a more powerful and fulfilling life.

How To Use The Law of Gender

Like the law of polarity and the law of rhythm, there really isn't any specific thing you can do to "use" the law of gender. The most important thing is knowing they are around, knowing they are present in your every day and start to notice them around you.

For example – if you get an idea, that is the feminine power (why some say you conceive an idea) at work. As you rationalize the idea and put it into action, that is the masculine energy at work.

When something drastic or emotional happens in your life, that initial rock of emotions is the feminine energy.

The masculine energy creates a plan to ride out the issue.

You need both the masculine and feminine in life. Literally, without the masculine and feminine, life would not exist!

Start looking for ways the law of gender is at play in your life – notice the soft yet emotional strength in the feminine power and the strong, determined power in the masculine energy.

www.ingramcontent.com/pod-product-compliance
Ingram Content Group UK Ltd.
Pitfield, Milton Keynes, MK11 3LW, UK
UKHW041956190726
13854UKWH00005B/2007

9 798886 295306